Outstanding Dissertations in the

COMPUTER SCIENCES

A Continuing Garland Research Series

Axiomatic Proof Techniques for Parallel Programs

Susan Speer Owicki

Garland Publishing, Inc.
New York & London, 1980

Library of Congress Cataloging in Publication Data

Owicki, Susan Speer.
Axiomatic proof techniques for parallel programs.

(Outstanding dissertations in the computer sciences)
Originally presented as the author's thesis, Cornell University, 1975.
Bibliography: p.
1. Parallel processing (Electronic computers)
2. Computer programs—Verification. I. Title.
II. Series.
QA76.6.093 1980 001.6'42 79-50560
ISBN 0-8240-4413-4

All volumes in this series are printed on acid-free, 250-year-life paper.

Printed in the United States of America

AXIOMATIC PROOF TECHNIQUES FOR PARALLEL PROGRAMS[+]

Susan Speer Owicki

TR 75-251

July 1975

Department of Computer Science
Cornell University
Ithaca, NY 14853

[+] This research was partially supported by National Science Foundation grant GJ-42512.

ACKNOWLEDGMENTS

I am deeply indebted to Professor David Gries, my thesis advisor. He was a constant source of encouragement and advice, and taught me a great deal about the organization and presentation of information.

Thanks also go to Professors Juris Hartmannis and James Bramble for serving on my special committee. I had many valuable discussions of parallel processing with Professor Charles Moore, and of logic with Professor Robert Constable and Marvin Solomon.

The superb typing of this thesis is the work of Mrs. Caroline Marold, who did much to improve its layout and appearance.

Finally, I am very grateful to my husband Jack for his help and support throughout this research.

TABLE OF CONTENTS

AXIOMATIC PROOF TECHNIQUES FOR PARALLEL PROGRAMS

Susan Speer Owicki, Ph.D.
Cornell University 1975

This thesis presents an axiomatic method for proving certain correctness properties of parallel programs. Axioms and inference rules for partial correctness are given for two parallel programming languages: the General Parallel Language and the Restricted Parallel Language. The General language is flexible enough to represent most standard synchronizers (e.g., semaphores, events), so that programs using these synchronizers may be verified using the GPL deductive system. However, proofs for GPL programs are in general quite complex. The Restricted language reduces this complexity by requiring shared variables to be protected by critical sections, so that only one process at a time has access to them. This discipline does not significantly reduce the power of the language, and it greatly simplifies the process of program verification.

Although the axioms and inference rules are primarily intended for proofs of partial correctness, there are a number of other important properties of parallel programs. We give some practical techniques which use information obtained from a partial correctness proof to derive other correctness properties, including program termination, mutual exclusion, and freedom from deadlock. A number of examples of such proofs are given.

Finally, the axioms and inference rules are shown to be consistent and complete (in a special sense) with respect to an interpretive model of parallel execution. Thus the deductive system gives an accurate description of program execution and is powerful enough to yield a proof of any true partial correctness formula.

CHAPTER 1

INTRODUCTION

1.1. Introduction.

The purpose of this thesis is to present an axiomatic method for proving certain properties of parallel programs. The most fundamental property is partial correctness: a program is partially correct if it either computes the required result or fails to terminate. Total correctness includes the requirement that the program terminates. Hoare [Ho69] has developed axioms and inference rules for proving the partial correctness of sequential programs written in an Algol-like syntax, and with certain adaptations this deductive system can be used to establish total correctness (Manna [Ma74]). Its extension to parallel programs (Hoare [Ho72]) is the basis of the work in this thesis.

The importance of correctness proofs for sequential programs has long been recognized. The advocates of structured programming have argued that a well structured program should be easy to prove correct, and that programs should be written with a correctness proof in mind. The need is even greater with parallel programs. If several processes are executed in parallel, their results can depend on the unpredictable order in which actions from different processes are executed. For example the two simple processes below can interact in six different ways to produce four different values for y .

```
process 1: x:=1 ;          process 2: x:=2 ;
           y:=x+1 ;                   y:=5*x ;
```

Such complexity greatly increases the probability that the programmer will make mistakes. Even worse, the mistakes may not be detected during program testing, since the particular interactions in which the errors are visible may not occur. It is important to structure parallel programs in a way which eliminates some of this complexity, and to verify their correctness with proofs as well as by program testing.

A number of methods have been used in proofs for parallel programs. The most common is reliance on informal arguments -- a risky business given the complexity of parallel program interactions. More formal approaches have included application of Scott's mathematical semantics (Cadiou and Levy [Ca73]), Lipton's reduction method [Li74b], and Rosen's Church-Rosser approach [Ro74]. The work which is most directly related to this thesis is based on Floyd's inductive assertion method [Fl67] for sequential programs. In this approach assertions are attached to the arcs of a flowchart, and a verification condition is developed which guarantees that whenever control follows an arc the corresponding assertion is true. This verification condition for sequential programs is fairly simple, but for parallel programs it can be quite complex. Ashcroft and Manna [As71] express a parallel program as a nondeterministic sequential program. This gives a simple verification condition, but the number of assertions is an exponential function of the number of program statements. In [As73], Ashcroft uses a similar technique, but argues that in practice the number of distinct assertions will not be too large. Lauer [La73] and Newton [Ne74] attach assertions to control points in the flowchart of each parallel process. This makes the number of assertions linear in the size of the program. Unfortunately, the verification condition becomes more complicated, because it is necessary to check that the statements in one process do not invalidate the assertions in another. The result is that the complexity of the proof grows as the square of the program size, but in practice all but a few of the checks are trivial.

All of the inductive assertion methods deal with flowcharts, but they can be used as the basis of an axiomatic description of parallel programming languages. Instead of having assertions attached to points in a flowchart, they are applied to program statements according to a set of axioms and inference rules. Working with language statements rather than flowcharts makes it easier to enforce restrictions which make programs intellectually manageable; it is even possible to completely eliminate the exponential factor mentioned above. The axioms and inference rules provide a sound formal technique for proving partial correctness, but they are also intuitive enough to be used as the basis of reliable informal proofs. One of their main advantages is that they give guidance in structuring programs in a way that makes them easy to understand as well as to prove correct.

Although the deductive system described above is designed for proving partial correctness, it can also be used to demonstrate other important properties of parallel programs. For example, mutual exclusion, the property that two or more processes cannot execute certain statements at the same time, can be proved using axiomatic techniques and certain theorems about program execution. Similarly, we can find practical, sufficient conditions, in terms of the axioms, for showing that all processes cannot become blocked (deadlocked). These results, combined with Manna's work, make it possible to prove program termination in many cases.

There are two questions which naturally occur in considering an axiomatic semantics for a programming language. The first is: do the axioms and inference rules correctly describe the results of executing a program? The second: are they powerful enough to make it possible to prove all true statements about a program? A partial answer can be obtained by defining an interpretive model of program execution and then asking the questions with respect to that model. The first then becomes: do the axioms and inference rules correctly describe the results of executing a program under our model? If they do, the deductive system is said to be consistent with the model. It has been proved that Hoare's sequential deductive system is consistent with several models of program execution (Cook [Co75], Hoare and Lauer [Ho74b]). The second question becomes: is the deductive system powerful enough to prove everything which is true about program execution in this model? If so, it is said to be complete with respect to the model. Cook [Co75] has recently proved that the sequential axioms and inference rules are complete in a restricted sense which will be discussed later. In this thesis, we will show that the axioms given for parallel processing are consistent and complete in Cook's sense for one model of parallel execution.

1.2. Outline of the Thesis.

Chapter 2 is a review of Hoare's axioms and inference rules for a sequential programming language (SL). There are no new results here, but many of the concepts needed for parallel programs are introduced at this time. In particular, an interpretive model for sequential execution is developed which is later extended to provide for parallel computations.

In Chapter 3 we move on to discuss parallel programs. The language presented here is called the general parallel language (GPL) because it is powerful enough to represent most of the primitive operations suggested for synchronizing parallel processes (e.g., events, Dijkstra's semaphores). The deductive system and the model from Chapter 2 are extended to include parallel operations.

In Chapter 4 we consider a parallel programming language and deductive system suggested by Hoare. This restricted parallel language (RPL) is more highly structured than the one given in Chapter 3, and this greatly simplifies program proofs. In fact, the size of the proofs again becomes linear in the size of the program, as it is for sequential programs. Once again the interpretive model defined in Chapter 2 can be extended to cover the new language.

Chapter 5 discusses methods for proving other properties besides partial correctness. Using both the deductive system and the interpretive model of program execution it is possible to derive easily-verified sufficient conditions for guaranteeing mutual exclusion, termination, and safety from blocking.

Chapter 6 considers the relationship between the deductive and interpretive semantics presented in earlier chapters. The two methods are shown to be consistent for all three languages, and the deductive system for RPL is shown to be complete with respect to the interpreter.

Finally, Chapter 7 summarizes our results and suggests extensions and areas for future work.

CHAPTER 2

SEQUENTIAL PROGRAMS

We begin our study of parallel programs by describing a simple sequential language which will be the basis of our two parallel languages. The sequential language is a fragment of Algol, for which Hoare has given a set of axioms and inference rules. We define a simple interpreter for this language and sketch a proof that it is consistent with Hoare's deductive system. Chapters 3 and 4 will extend the language to include constructs for parallel programming.

2.1. The Sequential Programming Language (SL).

The programming language SL contains five statements:

1. assignment -- x:=E where x is a variable and E is an expression
2. null -- ;
3. compound -- <u>begin</u> $S_1;\ldots;S_n$ <u>end</u>
4. alternation -- <u>if</u> B <u>then</u> S_1 <u>else</u> S_2
5. iteration -- <u>while</u> B <u>do</u> S_1

where B is a Boolean expression and the S_i are statements.

Note that there are no declaration statements; it is assumed that all variables are globally defined. This simplifies the axioms and the model of program execution, but declarations could be included without changing any of the results. Ses Lauer [La71] and Cook [Co75] for the treatment of variable declarations.

We also choose not to specify the syntax of expressions. Most of the time we will use the standard Algol syntax for integer and logical expressions, but the techniques apply equally well to other data types and operations.

At times it will be useful to speak of the relation between a statement and the statements it contains.

2.1. Definition: Let S be an SL statement. The primary components of S are

1) none if S is an assignment or null
2) $S_1, S_2, \ldots, S_n$ if S is **begin** $S_1; \ldots; S_n$ **end**
3) S_1, S_2 if S is **if** B **then** S_1 **else** S_2
4) S_1 if S is **while** B **do** S_1 .

The proper components of S are the primary components of S and their proper components. The components of S are S itself and its proper components.

2.2. The Deductive Semantics.

Hoare [Ho69] has developed axioms and inference rules for proving the partial correctness of sequential programs. He uses the formula {P} S {Q} to represent the partial correctness of the program S with respect to assertions P and Q . This means that if P is true of the program variables before executing S , and if S terminates, Q will be true of the program variables after execution of S is complete. P and Q must be formulas of the first-order predicate calculus. For example the formula $\{x \leq y\}\ z := (x+y)/2\ \{x \leq z \leq y\}$ expresses the fact that if $x \leq y$ when the statement $z := (x+y)/2$ begins, $x \leq z \leq y$ will be true when (and if) the statement finishes.

Table 2.1 gives two axiom schemas (A1 and A2) and four inference rules (A0, A3-A5) for sequential programs. The notation

$$\frac{P_1, P_2, \ldots, P_n}{P}$$

for inference rules means that P can be proved by proving each of the P_i and then applying the inference rule.

A1-A5 correspond to the five kinds of program statements. Rule A0 requires some additional comment. The notation $P \vdash Q$ means that it is possible to prove Q using P as an assumption. The deductive system to be used in proving Q from P is not given; it could be any system which is valid for the data types and operations used in the programming language. For example, if the programming language contains natural numbers and the operations + and * , the deductive system could be based on Peano's axioms.

Figure 2.1 gives an example of a partial correctness proof. The program <u>power</u> computes $z=x^y$ if $y \geq 0$ (x and y are integers). The partial correctness condition is

$$\{y \geq 0\}\ \text{power}\ \{z=x^y\}\ .$$

Lines 1-2 describe the statement labelled init 1, lines 3-4 describe init 2, and lines 6-10 describe the loop. Finally, the effect of the three statements together is given in line 11.

A0 consequence $$\frac{\{P'\}\ S\ \{Q'\}\ ,\ P \vdash P'\ ,\ Q' \vdash Q}{\{P\}\ S\ \{Q\}}$$

A1 assignment $\{P^x_E\}\ x{:=}E\ \{P\}$

where P^x_E represents the result of substituting E for each free occurrence of x in P . e.g., if P is $(a \geq 0 \vee b=1)$, P^a_{a+b} is $(a+b \geq 0 \vee b=1)$.

A2 null $\{P\}\ ;\ \{P\}$

A3 composition $$\frac{\{P_1\}\ S_1\ \{P_2\}\ ,\ \{P_2\}\ S_2\ \{P_3\},\ldots,\{P_n\}\ S_n\ \{P_{n+1}\}}{\{P_1\}\ \underline{\text{begin}}\ S_1;\ldots;S_n\ \underline{\text{end}}\ \{P_{n+1}\}}$$

A4 alternation $$\frac{\{P \wedge B\}\ S_1\ \{Q\}\ ,\ \{P \wedge \neg B\}\ S_2\ \{Q\}}{\{P\}\ \underline{\text{if}}\ B\ \underline{\text{then}}\ S_1\ \underline{\text{else}}\ S_2\ \{Q\}}$$

A5 iteration $$\frac{\{P \wedge B\}\ S_1\ \{P\}}{\{P\}\ \underline{\text{while}}\ B\ \underline{\text{do}}\ S_1\ \{P \wedge \neg B\}}$$

Table 2.1. Axioms and Inference Rules for Sequential Programs.

```
power: begin  init1: z:=1;  init2: temp:=y;
              loop: while  temp>0  do
                        mult: begin  upz: z:=x*z;
                                     downtemp: temp:=temp-1
                              end
       end
```

1. $\{y \geq 0 \wedge 1=1\}$ z:=1 $\{y \geq 0 \wedge z=1\}$ A1

2. $\{y \geq 0\}$ z:=1 $\{y \geq 0 \wedge z=1\}$ 1, A0, using $y \geq 0 \vdash (y \geq 0 \wedge 1=1)$

3. $\{y \geq 0 \wedge z=1 \wedge y=y\}$ temp:=y $\{y \geq 0 \wedge z=1 \wedge temp=y\}$ A1

4. $\{y \geq 0 \wedge z=1\}$ temp:=y $\{temp \geq 0 \wedge z=x^{y-temp}\}$ 3, A0

5. $\{temp-1 \geq 0 \wedge x*z=x^{y-(temp-1)}\}$ z:=x*z $\{temp-1 \geq 0 \wedge z=x^{y-(temp-1)}\}$ A1

6. $\{temp \geq 0 \wedge z=x^{y-temp} \wedge temp>0\}$ z:=x*z $\{temp-1 \geq 0 \wedge z=x^{y-(temp-1)}\}$ 5, A0

7. $\{temp-1 \geq 0 \wedge z=x^{y-(temp-1)}\}$ temp:=temp-1 $\{temp \geq 0 \wedge z=x^{y-temp}\}$ A1

8. $\{temp \geq 0 \wedge z=x^{y-temp} \wedge temp>0\}$ mult: <u>begin</u> z:=x*z; temp:=temp-1 <u>end</u>
   $\{temp \geq 0 \wedge z=x^{y-temp}\}$ 6, 7, A3

9. $\{temp \geq 0 \wedge z=x^{y-temp}\}$ loop: <u>while</u> temp>0 <u>do</u> mult
   $\{temp \geq 0 \wedge z=x^{y-temp} \wedge \neg(temp>0)\}$ 8, A5

10. $\{temp \geq 0 \wedge z=x^{y-temp}\}$ loop $\{z=x^y\}$ 9, A0

11. $\{y \geq 0\}$ power $\{z=x^y\}$ 2, 4, 10, A3

Figure 2.1. A Formal Partial Correctness Proof.

Of course this is a very tedious proof of a simple result -- much like an algebraic proof that $(a+b)(a+b) = a^2 + 2ab + b^2$ when every use of the commutative and distributive laws is presented. Figure 2.2 contains a more informal version of the same proof -- assertions enclosed in braces {} are interspersed with the program, while some of the proof steps are combined or omitted. Most of our proofs will be presented in this style. When proving programs correct in a practical manner, we use the formal methods only in the difficult parts and use less formal techniques on the simple parts. The most difficult part of sequential programs is iterative loops, and it is usually worthwhile to carefully apply inference rule A5 to each <u>while</u> statement. On the other hand, assignment statements and <u>begin</u> ... <u>end</u> blocks are relatively simple and can often be treated informally.

In Figure 2.2 the assertion $P = \{temp>0 \wedge z=x^{y-temp}\}$ appears just before statement mult. This corresponds to the fact that P must hold whenever mult is ready to be executed in a computation which starts with $y \geq 0$. P can be called a <u>pre-condition</u> of mult, and $Q = \{temp \geq 0 \wedge z=x^{y-temp}\}$ is a <u>post-condition</u>. A proof of {P} S {Q} gives at least one pre- and post-condition for each component of S . For example, line 8 in the proof of $\{y \geq 0\}$ power $\{z=x^y\}$ gives the pre- and post-conditions for mult cited above. Lines 9 and 10 give two post-conditions for loop, namely $\{temp \geq 0 \wedge z=x^{y-temp} \wedge \neg(temp>0)\}$ and $\{z=x^y\}$.

At times it will be useful to single out a particular pre- (or post-) condition of a statement S and call it pre(S) (or post(S)).

```
{y≥0}

 power: begin  z:=1; temp:=y;

               {temp≥0 ∧ z=x^(y-temp)}

               loop: while  temp>0  do

                     {temp>0 ∧ z=x^(y-temp)}

                     mult: begin  z:=x*z; temp:=temp-1 end

                     {temp≥0 ∧ z=x^(y-temp)}

               {temp≥0 ∧ z=x^(y-temp) ∧ ¬(temp>0)}

        end

{z=x^y}
```

Figure 2.2. An Informal Partial Correctness Proof.

Given pre(S') and post(S') for each component S' of S , it is possible to reconstruct a proof of {P} S {Q} , if pre(S') and post(S') satisfy certain requirements.

2.2. Definition: Let pre and post be functions which map components of S to assertions. Then pre and post are assertion functions for {P} S {Q} iff they obey the following restrictions for each component S' of S :

1) $P \vdash pre(S)$ and $post(S) \vdash Q$
2) if S' is x:=E , $pre(S') \vdash post(S')^x_E$
3) if S' is null, $pre(S') \vdash post(S')$
4) if S' is begin $S_1;\ldots;S_n$ end
   a) $pre(S') \vdash pre(S_1)$ and $post(S_n) \vdash post(S')$
   b) $post(S_i) \vdash pre(S_{i+1})$ $i=1,\ldots,n-1$
5) if S' is if B then S_1 else S_2
   a) $pre(S') \wedge B \vdash pre(S_1)$ and $pre(S') \wedge \neg B \vdash pre(S_2)$
   b) $post(S_1) \vdash post(S')$ and $post(S_2) \vdash post(S')$
6) if S' is while B do S_1
   a) $pre(S') \wedge B \vdash pre(S_1)$
   b) $post(S_1) \vdash pre(S')$
   c) $pre(S') \wedge \neg B \vdash post(S')$

A proof of {P} S {Q} and a pair of assertion functions for {P} S {Q} are very closely related. Given either one, the other can be derived as shown in the next two theorems. In general, we will first give a partial correctness proof, then derive assertion functions from it.

The assertion functions are useful in proving the consistency of the deductive system and in discussing various properties of parallel programs in Chapter 5. The key point is that pre(S') must hold whenever S' is ready to execute and post(S') must hold whenever S' is finished.

2.3. Theorem: If pre and post are assertion functions for {P} S {Q} , it is possible to prove {pre(S')} S' {post(S')} for each component S' of S .

Proof: By induction on the structure of S' . Two cases will be given; the rest are similar.

Case 1: S' is x:=E

1. $\{post(S')^x_E\}$ S' {post(S')} A1
2. {pre(S')} S' {post(S')} 1, A0, and requirement 2 for pre and post

Case 2: S' is while B do S_1

1. $\{pre(S_1)\}\ S_1\ \{post(S_1)\}$ induction
2. $\{pre(S') \wedge B\}\ S_1\ \{pre(S')\}$ 1, A0, requirements 6a, 6b
3. $\{pre(S')\}\ S'\ \{pre(S') \wedge \neg B\}$ 2, A5
4. {pre(S')} S' {post(S')} 3, A0, and requirement 6c

2.4. Theorem: If there is a proof of {P} S {Q} , there are assertion functions pre and post for {P} S {Q} .

Proof: Pre and post can be obtained from the proof; they will be defined in such a way that {pre(S')} S' {post(S')} is a line in the proof, for each component S' of S . Since the proof may contain more than one line which refers to S' , we must specify which line is chosen to give pre(S') and post(S'). We eliminate all lines which do not contribute to the proof of {P} S {Q} (for example, line 1 in the proof of $\{x \le y\}$ z:=(x+y)/2 $\{x \le z \le y\}$ below).

1. $\{(x+y)/2>0\}$ z:=(x+y)/2 $\{z>0\}$ A1
2. $\{x \le (x+y)/2 \le y\}$ z:=(x+y)/2 $\{x \le z \le y\}$ A1
3. $\{x \le y\}$ z:=(x+y)/2 $\{x \le z \le y\}$ 2, A0

In this reduced proof there will be one line which refers to S' and uses one of rules A1 to A5. It is from this line that we choose pre(S') and post(S'). Any other lines with the form {P'} S' {Q'} must be derived from {pre(S')} S' {post(S')} by one or more applications of A0. Thus, $P' \vdash pre(S')$ and $post(S') \vdash Q'$.

Now we must verify that pre and post satisfy Definition 2.2. Two representative cases will be considered. If S' is x:=E , {pre(S')} x:=E {post(S')} is an application of A1. Thus, pre(S') = $post(S')^x_E$ and 1 is satisfied. If S' is <u>while</u> B <u>do</u> S_1 , {pre(S')} S' {post(S')} is an application of A5. This implies that $post(S') = (pre(S') \wedge \neg B)$, satisfying 6c, and that $\{pre(S') \wedge B\}$ S_1 {pre(S')} has been proved. Since $\{pre(S') \wedge B\}$ S_1 {pre(S')} is a line in the proof, $pre(S') \wedge B \vdash pre(S_1)$ and $post(S_1) \vdash pre(S')$, satisfying 6a and 6b.

<u>2.3. The Interpretive Model.</u>

In the last section, the semantics of the Algol fragment SL was defined by axioms and inference rules at a very abstract level. This section uses an operational approach, in which the effect of a program is described by giving an interpreter for the programming language. This interpretive model is consistent with the deductive system. It will be used extensively in Chapter 5 when discussing mutual exclusion and blocking, which cannot be expressed directly in terms of partial correctness.

The interpreter for an SL program consists of a set of states and a state-to-state transition function. A program state has two components -- a control, which gives the next instruction to be executed, and a variable state which gives the current value of each variable.

2.5. Definition: A program state for a program S is an ordered pair, $s=(c,v)$ in which

1) the variable state v is a function from variable names of S to values.
2) the control state c is a tree in which every node is labelled with a statement from S in such a way that if S_1 is a component of S_2, and S_1 and S_2 both appear in c, S_1 is a descendant of S_2. (Here each node is considered a descendant of itself.)

The variable state v is a function defined on all program variables, although the value returned for an uninitialized variable is not specified. The notation $E[s]$ will be used for the value of expression E in state $s=(c,v)$. Thus, if v assigns 0 to x, (x+1)[s]=1 . For an assertion P we say P is true in s iff P[s]=true .

The control state for a sequential program is a degenerate tree in which each node has zero or one sons. The single leaf is the next statement to be executed. In order to simplify notation we will assign a unique label to each statement and use the statement and its label interchangeably. Figure 2.3 contains examples of states for the program power of Figure 2.1. Note that the definition of control state guarantees that no statement appears more than once in the tree. For S is a component of itself, and if S appears at nodes m and n , m must be a descendant of n and vice versa. So m=n .

The execution of a statement can affect both components of the program state. The control is modified by replacing a leaf by a (possibly empty) tree.

<u>2.6. Definition</u>: If t and t' are trees, and n a leaf in t , <u>replace(t,n,t')</u> is the tree obtained by replacing n by t' in t .

<u>Example</u>: t =

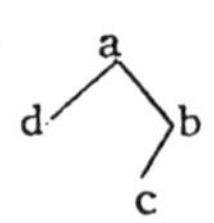

t' =

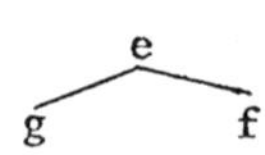

replace(t,d,t') =

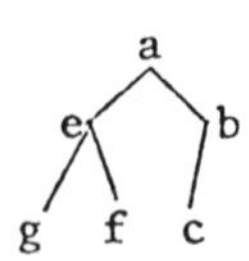

replace(t,c,Γ) =

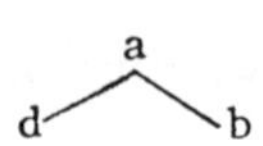

where Γ is the empty tree.

c_0 = . power

$v_0(x)=2$, $v_0(y)=1$, $v_0(z)=?$, $v_0(temp)=?$

a. $s_0 = (c_0, v_0)$

c_1 = loop | init2 | init1

$v_1(x)=2$, $v_1(y)=1$, $v_1(z)=?$, $v_1(temp)=?$

b. s_1 = next(s_0,power)

c_2 = loop | init2

$v_2(x)=2$, $v_2(y)=1$, $v_2(z)=1$, $v_2(temp)=?$

c. s_2 = next(s_1,init1)

c_3 = . loop

$v_3(x)=2$, $v_3(y)=1$, $v_3(z)=1$, $v_3(temp)=1$

d. s_3 = next(s_2,init2)

c_4 = loop | mult

$v_4(x)=2$, $v_4(y)=1$, $v_4(z)=1$, $v_4(temp)=1$

e. s_4 = next(s_3,loop)

c_5 = loop | downtemp | upz

$v_5(x)=2$, $v_5(y)=1$, $v_5(z)=1$, $v_5(temp)=1$

f. s_5 = next(s_4,mult)

c_6 = loop | downtemp

$v_6(x)=2$, $v_6(y)=1$, $v_6(z)=2$, $v_6(temp)=1$

g. s_6 = next(s_5,upz)

c_7 = . loop

$v_7(x)=2$, $v_7(y)=1$, $v_7(z)=2$, $v_7(temp)=0$

h. s_7 = next(s_6,downtemp)

c_8 = Γ

$v_8(x)=2$, $v_8(y)=1$, $v_8(z)=2$, $v_8(temp)=0$

i. s_8 = next(s_7,loop)

Figure 2.3. A Sequence of Program States for the Program Power of Figure 2.1.

The variable state can be modified by an assignment statement. The new variable state will be the same as the old, except at the variable which received a value.

2.7. Definition: If v is a variable state function and E is an expression, $v\langle a|E\rangle$ is a new variable state function defined by

$$x[v\langle a|E\rangle] = x[v] \quad \text{if} \quad x \neq a$$
$$= E[v] \quad \text{if} \quad x = a \; .$$

The effect of each type of statement is defined by the state transition function "next". An assignment statement changes both the control and the variable state; all others change only the control. Note that if S is a compound statement (begin ... end, if or while), next(s,S) describes the effect of starting S in state s rather than the effect of a complete execution of S.

2.8. Definition: The state transition function

$$\text{next: \{program states\}} \times \text{\{statements\}} \rightarrow \text{\{program states\}}$$

is given by

$$\text{next}((c,v),S) = (c',v') \quad \text{if } S \text{ is a leaf in } c$$
$$= \text{undefined} \quad \text{otherwise}$$

where

$$v' = v\langle x|E\rangle \quad \text{if } S \text{ is } x{:=}E$$
$$= v \quad \text{otherwise}$$

and

$$
\begin{aligned}
c' &= \text{replace}(c,S,\Gamma) \quad \text{if } S \text{ is assignment or null } (\Gamma \text{ is the empty tree}) \\
&= \text{replace}\left(c,S,\begin{array}{l} S_n \\ S_{n-1} \\ \vdots \\ S_1 \end{array}\right) \quad \text{if } S \text{ is } \underline{\text{begin}}\ S_1;\ldots;S_n\ \underline{\text{end}} \\
&= \text{replace}(c,S,S_1) \quad \text{if } S \text{ is } \underline{\text{if}}\ B\ \underline{\text{then}}\ S_1\ \underline{\text{else}}\ S_2 \text{ and } B[s]=\text{true} \\
&= \text{replace}(c,S,S_2) \quad \text{if } S \text{ is } \underline{\text{if}}\ B\ \underline{\text{then}}\ S_1\ \underline{\text{else}}\ S_2 \text{ and } B[s]=\text{false} \\
&= \text{replace}\left(c,S,\begin{array}{l} S \\ S_1 \end{array}\right) \quad \text{if } S \text{ is } \underline{\text{while}}\ B\ \underline{\text{do}}\ S_1 \text{ and } B[s]=\text{true} \\
&= \text{replace}(c,S,\Gamma) \quad \text{if } S \text{ is } \underline{\text{while}}\ B\ \underline{\text{do}}\ S_1 \text{ and } B[s]=\text{false}.
\end{aligned}
$$

<u>Example</u>: See Figure 2.3.

We have not described the effect of next if an arithmetic or Boolean expression can't be evaluated for some reason (for example, it involves division by zero or an uninitialized variable). There are two ways in which the interpreter could respond in such a situation. One is to stop execution; the other is to choose some arbitrary value for the expression, for example, 0 for numeric expressions and true for Boolean expressions. In the interpreter we will follow the second alternative. For example, the effect of executing the statement $x:=4/0$ is to assign 0 to x. The axioms and inference rules can be made to reflect this choice by assigning the same value as the interpreter to expressions which are normally considered undefined. For the statement $x:=4/0$, A1 can be applied to give a proof of $\{4/0=4/0\}\ x:=4/0\ \{x=4/0\}$ or $\{\text{true}\}\ x:=4/0\ \{x=0\}$. The deductive system used in the rule of consequence (A0) must be chosen in a way which is consistent with the assignment of values to expressions like x/0 , but this should cause no problems.

Note that {true} x:=4/0 {x=0} is also consistent with an implementation in which execution stops on encountering the illegal division, since in that case the statement does not terminate, and {P} S {Q} is true for any P and Q .

For sequential programs there is only one order in which statements can be executed, but for parallel programs this is no longer the case. In order to provide a basis for the parallel interpreter, we define a "computation", which records the order of statement execution, and then define some useful properties of computations.

2.9. Definition: A computation α for program S beginning with variable state v_0 is a sequence of statements $S_1\ S_2 \ldots S_n$ such that if $s_0 = (S, v_0)$ the sequence of states $s_i = \text{next}(s_{i-1}, S_i)$ is defined, i.e., S_i is a leaf in s_{i-1} . If $\alpha = S_1 \ldots S_n$ is a computation, let $\text{value}(s_0, \alpha) = s_n$. If P is an assertion we say P is true after α iff $P[\text{value}(s_0,\alpha)]=\text{true}$.

Example: From Figure 2.3, α = (power, init1, init2, loop, mult, upz, downtemp, loop) is a computation for power beginning with state v_0 . $\text{Value}(s_0,\alpha) = s_8$, $z[\text{value}(s_0,\alpha)] = 2$, and $z=x^y$ is true after α .

2.10. Definition: Statement S is ready to execute after computation α iff S is a leaf in the control of $\text{value}(s_0,\alpha)$.

Examples: From Figure 2.3, init1 is ready to execute after α = (power) and init2 is ready to execute after α = (power, init1).

2.11. Definition: If α is a computation for S and S' is a component of S , α finishes S' iff

1) S' is an assignment or null statement, and S' is the last statement in α , or
2) S' is <u>while</u> B <u>do</u> S_1 , S' is the last statement in α , and B is false after α , or
3) S' is <u>begin</u> $S_1;\ldots;S_n$ <u>end</u> and α finishes S_n , or
4) S' is <u>if</u> B <u>then</u> S_1 <u>else</u> S_2 and α finishes S_1 or S_2 .

Example: From Figure 2.3f, α = (power, init1, init2, loop, body, upz, downtemp) finishes downtemp and body.

2.12. Definition: α executes S iff α is a computation for S which finishes S .

Example: From Figure 2.3i, α = (power, init1, init2, loop, body, upz, downtemp, loop) executes power.

Note that for a given initial state s_0 there is at most one computation which executes S . This is not true for parallel programs. If S contains an infinite loop, no computation executes S .

2.13. Definition: execute(s,S) = value(s,α) if S is ready to execute in s and α is a computation which executes S from state s . If S is not ready to execute in s , or no such α exists, execute(s,S) is undefined.

This completes the description of the interpreter for sequential programs. In Chapter 3 it will be extended to include parallel programs.

2.4. Consistency of the Deductive System and the Interpreter.

Sections 2.2 and 2.3 specify the semantics of the language SL in two different ways. In this section, we state a theorem to the effect that the two methods are consistent. To keep the reader from getting bogged down in details, we only sketch the proof here, delaying a complete presentation until Chapter 6. Hopefully, both methods correspond well enough with the reader's intuitive idea of program execution that he is willing to believe they are not contradictory.

In order to show that the deductive system and the interpretive model are consistent, we must show that {P} S {Q} can only be proved when it is true for the interpreter.

2.14. Definition: {P} S {Q} is true for the interpreter iff any computation α which executes S from state s_0 with $P[s_0]$ = true has $Q[\text{value}(s_0,\alpha)]$ = true.

In order to show that a proof of {P} S {Q} implies that {P} S {Q} is true in the model, we first derive a stronger result using assertion functions.

2.15. Theorem: If pre and post are assertion functions for {P} S {Q}, S' is a component of S, and α is a computation for S from a state s_0 with $P[s_0]$ = true, then

1) if S' is ready to execute after α, pre(S') is true after α;
2) if α finishes S', post(S') is true after α.

Proof: The proof uses induction on the length of α . If α is empty, 1) is satisfied because P is true for s_0 and $P \vdash pre(S)$. 2) does not apply.

For $\alpha = \alpha'T$, pre(T) is true after α' by induction. Proving that 1) and 2) are satisfied for $\alpha'T$ is a straightforward but tedious application of the definition of assertion functions. The details are given in Chapter 6.

2.16. Corollary: If {P} S {Q} can be proved, it is true for the interpreter.

Proof: By Theorem 2.4, there are assertion functions pre and post for {P} S {Q} . Now suppose α executes S from state s_0 with $P[s_0]$ = true. Then by the last theorem, $post(S)[value(s_0,\alpha)]$ = true , and $Q[value(s_0,\alpha)]$ = true since $post(S) \vdash Q$. So {P} S {Q} is true for the interpreter.

This finishes our review of sequential programs. In the next chapter the axioms and the model are extended to parallel programs.

CHAPTER 3

PARALLEL PROGRAMS

In this chapter we introduce parallel programs by extending the language of Chapter 2. Two new statements will be added, cobegin - coend to initiate parallel execution, and a synchronization statement called await to coordinate processes executing in parallel. The await statement is very flexible -- in fact it is too general to be implemented in an efficient way. It is included here because it can be used to represent many standard synchronizing primitives, such as events and semaphores. Thus, the proof techniques for GPL can be applied to programs which use these synchronizers.

The language in this chapter is relatively primitive and provides only limited facilities for structuring the interactions of processes using shared variables. We will see that the axioms for the parallel and synchronization statements are easy to understand; they state quite easily when we can know that parallel processes don't "interfere" with each other. But proofs using them will be difficult because of the exponential number of checks that may be necessary to satisfy this noninterference criterion. In Chapter 4, we present another language in which the use of shared variables is closely regulated; this makes proofs of program correctness much simpler. However, no such language is yet in use (see Brinch Hansen [Br74]) so the results in this chapter are more readily applicable to programs written in the languages which are currently available.

3.1. The General Parallel Language (GPL).

The language of this chapter is the sequential language of Chapter 2 plus two statements for parallel processing:

parallel execution -- cobegin $S_1//\ldots//S_n$ coend

synchronization -- await B then S_1

where S_i is a statement and B a Boolean expression. The first statement initiates parallel execution of $S_1 \ldots S_n$. When all of the S_i have finished, the parallel statement terminates and execution can proceed to the next statement. There are no restrictions on the way in which parallel execution is implemented; in particular nothing is assumed about the relative speeds of different S_i. The primary components of a cobegin ... coend statement are called parallel processes.

3.1. Definition: Components T_1 and T_2 of S are in *different processes* iff S contains a statement cobegin $S_1//\ldots//S_n$ coend with T_1 and T_2 components of different S_i. Otherwise, T_1 and T_2 are in the *same process*.

Note that according to this definition, the cobegin statement itself is in the same process as each of its components. A program can be visualized as one large process which may contain a number of different subprocesses. Since parallel statements can be nested, any process may contain subprocesses.

The second new statement, await B then S, is designed to provide synchronization between parallel processes, and it can only appear inside a cobegin statement. B is a Boolean expression, and S is a sequential statement which does not contain a cobegin or another await. When a process attempts to execute a synchronization statement, it is delayed until the condition B is true. Then the statement S is executed as an indivisible operation. If two or more processes are waiting for the same condition B , any one of them may be allowed to proceed when B becomes true. In some applications it is necessary to specify the order in which waiting processes are scheduled, for example on a first-come, first-served basis. For the problems discussed in this thesis, however, any scheduling rule at all is acceptable.

The await statement can be used to turn any sequential statement into an indivisible operation. This would be quite difficult to implement, and it is not suggested that the await statement is a desirable language feature. Instead it is presented because it can be used to represent a number of standard synchronizing primitives, such as Dijkstra's semaphore operations [Di68a].

A semaphore is an integer variable which can only be accessed by two operations, P and V .

P(sem): if sem>0 , sem:=sem-1 ; otherwise the process is suspended until sem>0 .

V(sem): sem:=sem+1 ;

The P and V operations are indivisible. They can be represented by synchronization statements as follows.

```
P(sem):  await sem>0 then sem:=sem-1 ;

V(sem):  await true then sem:=sem+1 ;
```

Lipton [Li74a] describes a number of generalizations of semaphores; all can be implemented using await statements.

In [Di68b], Dijkstra gives a slightly different definition of the semaphore operations.

P'(sem): sem:=sem-1 ; if sem<0 then the process is suspended on a queue associated with sem.

V'(sem): sem:=sem+1 ; if sem≤0 , awaken one of the processes on the semaphore's queue.

A possible implementation of these operations uses a Boolean array waiting, with one element for each process. Initially waiting[i]=false and waiting[i]=true → process i is on the queue.

```
P'(sem):  await true then
              begin  sem:=sem-1 ;
                     if  sem<0  then waiting[this process]:=true
              end
          await ¬waiting[this process]  then;

V'(sem):  await true then
              begin  sem:=sem+1 ;
                     if  sem≤0  then
```

```
                        begin choose  i  such that waiting[i]=true;
                              waiting[i]:=false;
                        end
                end
```

The operations P and V are an abstraction of P' and V'. There are some cases in which the effects of the two are not identical, but for the properties discussed in this thesis -- partial correctness, mutual exclusion, and deadlock -- the differences are irrelevant. See Lipton ([Li74a], Chapter 3) for a comparison of the two kinds of semaphore operations.

In order to prove the correctness of a program which uses semaphores, the semaphore operations can be replaced by the corresponding <u>await</u> statements. The result is an equivalent GPL program, which can be proved correct using the methods presented in this chapter. There are a number of other synchronization primitives which can be modelled using <u>await</u>, and the same technique can be applied to programs which contain such primitives. It is this flexibility which prompted the name "general parallel language".

3.2. The Interpretive Model.

The model of sequential program execution defined in Section 2.3 will now be extended to include parallelism. Recall that the interpreter had two components: a program state consisting of a control and a variable state, and a state transition function "next". The program state is defined exactly as before, although execution of a parallel program, unlike a sequential program, can lead to a control tree with more than one leaf. The function "next" must be extended to handle parallel and synchronization statements. next(s,S) is defined for all statements S which are ready to execute in s .

3.2. Definition: A statement S is current in the program state s=(c,v) iff S is a leaf in c .

3.3 Definition: S is ready to execute in state s=(c,v) iff S is current in s , and if S is await B then S_1 , B[s]=true.

Note that for sequential programs this reduces to the previous definition of "ready to execute".

3.4. Definition: The state transition function

next: {program states} $\times$ {statements} $\rightarrow$ {program states}

is given by

next((c,v),S) = undefined if S is not ready to execute in (c,v)

= execute((c',v),S_1) if S is await B then S_1 , where c' = replace(c,S,S_1) (see Definition 2.13)

= (c',v) if S is cobegin S_1//...//S_n coend, where c' is the tree obtained by deleting S in c and adding $S_1,\dots,S_n$ as sons of S's father, if any, and otherwise as roots of unconnected trees.

= (c',v') of Definition 2.8 if S is assignment, null, sequence, if, or while.

The definition next((c,v), <u>await</u> B <u>then</u> S_1) = execute((c',v),S_1) reflects the assumption that executing an <u>await</u> statement is an indivisible operation.

Figure 3.1 contains examples of the application of next. Note that in 3.1b the control state is actually a forest rather than a tree.

In this model parallel execution is simulated by nondeterminism. Instead of executing the processes in <u>cobegin</u> S_1//...//S_n <u>coend</u> simultaneously, it performs one action at a time, choosing nondeterministically which process to work on next. This means that in the program

```
newx: begin  x:=0 ;
             cobegin A: x:=x+1 // B: x:=x-1 coend
      end
```

either A or B is executed first -- they cannot overlap. This use of nondeterminism is standard in models of parallel execution, but it requires some justification. For example, the program above, executed by the interpreter, must finish with x=0 . A true parallel implementation might finish with x=1 if the actions took place as follows:

1. A evaluates x+1
2. B evaluates x-1
3. B stores -1 in x
4. A stores +1 in x

The discrepancy arises from the fact that the assignment x:=x+1 is treated as an indivisible operation by the interpreter, when in fact

```
S1: cobegin
       S2: begin  S3: x:=a*a;
                  S4: go := true;
           end
    //
       S5: begin  S6: y:=(a+1)*(a+1);
                  S7: await go then S8: sum:=x+y;
           end
    coend
```

$c_0 = \;\cdot\, S1$ $v_0(x)=?$ $v_0(y)=?$ $v_0(a)=0$ $v_0(go)=false$ $v_0(sum)=?$ a. $s_0 = (c_0, v_0)$	$c_1 = \;\cdot\, S2 \quad \cdot\, S5$ $v_1 = v_0$ b. $s_1 = next(s_0, S1)$	$c_2 = \;\cdot\, S2 \quad$ S7	S6 $v_2 = v_0$ c. $s_2 = next(s_1, S5)$	$c_3 = \;\cdot\, S2 \quad \cdot\, S7$ $v_3 = v_0\langle y \mid (a+1)*(a+1)\rangle$ d. $s_3 = next(s_2, S6)$
$c_4 =$ S4	S3 $\quad \cdot\, S7$ $v_4 = v_3$ e. $s_4 = next(s_3, S2)$	$c_5 = \;\cdot\, S4 \quad \cdot\, S7$ $v_5 = v_3\langle x \mid a*a\rangle$ f. $s_5 = next(s_4, S3)$	$c_6 = \;\cdot\, S7$ $v_6 = v_5\langle go \mid true\rangle$ g. $s_6 = next(s_5, S4)$	$c_7 = \Gamma$ $v_7(x)=0$ $v_7(y)=1$ $v_7(a)=0$ $v_7 = v_6\langle sum \mid x+y\rangle$ $v_7(go)=true$ $v_7(sum)=1$ h. $s_7 = next(s_6, S7)$

Figure 3.1. A Computation for the Parallel Program S1.

it is not. The solution is to restrict programs so that the assumption of indivisibility is a reasonable one. For example, if executing two actions simultaneously is the same as executing one and then the other, it is reasonable to treat them as indivisible. This certainly is the case if the actions do not have any variables in common. If they do, some care is required.

3.5. Definition: The variable x is shared in **cobegin** $S_1//\ldots//S_n$ **coend** if it is referenced in two or more of the S_i and changed (i.e., appears on the left side of an assignment) in at least one of them.

It is references to shared variables which cause problems when actions are treated as indivisible. But for actions which make at most one reference to a shared variable the assumption of indivisibility is reasonable. If two such actions are executed simultaneously, one of them must make the first access to the shared variable. The effect in parallel will be the same as if this action was executed first and followed by the other action.

In the interpreter, three kinds of actions are assumed to be indivisible:

1) an assignment statement
2) evaluating the Boolean expression in an **if** or **while**
3) synchronization statement.

3 is no problem, since a synchronization statement is intended to be indivisible in parallel execution. 1 and 2 are justified if each assignment and each **if** or **while** condition contains at most one reference

to a shared variable. We will only discuss programs which satisfy these requirements -- for such programs parallel and nondeterministic execution give the same results.

Because of the nondeterminism in the interpreter, a parallel program can be executed in a number of different ways. A computation gives one possible order in which statements can be executed. Computations and their properties are defined in much the same way as in Chapter 2.

3.6. Definition: A computation for program S beginning with variable state v_0 is a sequence of statements $S_1 \dots S_n$ such that if $s_0 = (S,v_0)$, the sequence of states $s_i = next(s_{i-1},S_i)$, $i=1 \dots n$ is defined, i.e., S_i is ready to execute after $S_1 \dots S_n$. In this case $value(s_0,\alpha)=s_n$, and an assertion P is true after α iff $P[value(s_0,\alpha)]=true$.

3.7. Definition: If α is a computation for S, and S' is a component of S, α finishes S' iff

1) S' is an assign, null, or await statement, and S' is the last statement of α from the same process as S', or
2) S' is while B do S_1, and S' is the last statement in α from the same process as S', and $B[value(s_0,\alpha)]=false$, or
3) S' is begin $S_1;\dots;S_n$ end and α finishes S_n, or
4) S' is if B then S_1 else S_2 and α finishes S_1 or S_2, or
5) S' is cobegin $S_1//\dots//S_n$ coend, and α finishes all the S_i $1 \leq i \leq n$.

3.8. Definition: α executes S iff α is a computation for S which finishes S .

At times it will be useful to speak of a statement being "in execution" in a computation.

3.9. Definition: S is in execution in a computation α iff a component of S is current after α . Thus, a statement is in execution from the time it is current until it has finished.

Finally, we review the definition of "true in the interpreter", which is the same for SL and GPL.

3.10. Definition: {P} S {Q} is true for the interpreter iff any computation α which executes S from state s_0 with $P[s_0]=true$ has $Q[value(s_0,\alpha)]=true$.

3.3. The Deductive System.

Table 3.1 gives the axioms and inference rules for GPL programs. They assume that the program obeys the restrictions on shared variables discussed in the last section. A0-A5 are identical to the rules for sequential programs. A6, the inference rule for synchronization statements, is quite straightforward. But rule A7 for parallel statements requires some discussion. It basically states that the effect of executing $S_1 \ldots S_n$ in parallel is the combined effect of executing each of the S_i by itself, provided that the processes do not interfere with each other. Of course the key to this statement is a definition of "interfere". One possibility is to require that S_i

A0	consequence	$$\frac{\{P'\}\ S\ \{Q'\}\ ,\quad P \vdash P'\ ,\quad Q' \vdash Q}{\{P\}\ S\ \{Q\}}$$
A1	assignment	$\{P^x_E\}\ x:=E\ \{P\}$
A2	null	$\{P\}\ ;\ \{P\}$
A3	composition	$$\frac{\{P_1\}\ S_1\ \{P_2\}\ ,\ \{P_2\}\ S_2\ \{P_3\},\ldots,\{P_n\}\ S_n\ \{P_{n+1}\}}{\{P_1\}\ \underline{\text{begin}}\ S_1;\ldots;S_n\ \underline{\text{end}}\ \{P_{n+1}\}}$$
A4	alternation	$$\frac{\{P \wedge B\}\ S_1\ \{Q\}\ ,\quad \{P \wedge \neg B\}\ S_2\ \{Q\}}{\{P\}\ \underline{\text{if}}\ B\ \underline{\text{then}}\ S_1\ \underline{\text{else}}\ S_2\ \{Q\}}$$
A5	iteration	$$\frac{\{P \wedge B\}\ S\ \{P\}}{\{P\}\ \underline{\text{while}}\ B\ \underline{\text{do}}\ S\ \{P \wedge \neg B\}}$$
A6	synchronization	$$\frac{\{P \wedge B\}\ S\ \{Q\}}{\{P\}\ \underline{\text{await}}\ B\ \underline{\text{then}}\ S\ \{Q\}}$$
A7	parallel	$$\frac{\{P_1\}\ S_1\ \{Q_1\},\ldots,\{P_n\}\ S_n\ \{Q_n\}}{\{P_1 \wedge\ldots\wedge P_n\}\ \underline{\text{cobegin}}\ S_1//\ldots//S_n\ \underline{\text{coend}}\ \{Q_1 \wedge\ldots\wedge Q_n\}}$$ provided $\{P_1\}\ S_1\ \{Q_1\}\ldots\{P_n\}\ S_n\ \{Q_n\}$ are interference-free

Table 3.1. Axioms and Inference Rules for GPL.

does not modify any shared variables. This makes the processes completely independent, but is too strong a requirement. A more useful restriction is that the assertions used in proving $\{P_i\}\ S_i\ \{Q_i\}$ are invariant as statements from other processes are executed. For example, the assertion $\{x \geq y\}$ in S_i remains true throughout the execution of $x:=x+1$ in S_j. The invariance of an assertion P over a statement S is expressed by the formula.

$\{P \wedge pre(S)\}\ S\ \{P\}$, where pre(S) is a pre-condition of S .

This invariance relation is the basis of the interference-free criterion. We will first define interference-free in terms of assertion functions and then relate it to program proofs.

<u>3.11. Definition</u>: Suppose S is a GPL program, and pre and post are functions which map components of S to assertions. They are <u>assertion functions</u> for {P} S {Q} iff they obey the following restrictions for each component S' of S .

1)-6) Same as Definition 2.2

7) if S' is <u>await</u> B <u>then</u> S_1

a) $pre(S') \wedge B \vdash pre(S_1)$

b) $post(S_1) \vdash post(S')$

8) if S' is <u>cobegin</u> $S_1 // \ldots // S_n$ <u>coend</u>

a) $pre(S') \vdash \bigwedge_{i=1}^{n} pre(S_i)$

b) $\bigwedge_{i=1}^{n} post(S_i) \vdash post(S')$

8) c) pre and post are interference-free for $S_1, \ldots, S_n$ i.e., if T is a component of S_i , and T' is an assignment or await in S_j , $(i \neq j)$, and neither T nor T' is a proper component of an await statement, then

$$\{pre(T) \wedge pre(T')\}\ T'\ \{pre(T)\}$$

$$\{post(T) \wedge pre(T')\}\ T'\ \{post(T)\}$$

can be proved.

The interference-free test in 8c guarantees that the assertions on S_i remain true as statements in S_j are executed. It is only necessary to check for invariance over assignment and synchronization statements, since all changes in data values take place in such statements. Proper components of await statements are not included in the tests because await statements are indivisible operations, and the state of variables at intermediate stages is not important.

The interference-free criterion for proofs, as required in A7, is defined in terms of assertion functions.

3.12. Definition: The formulas $\{P_1\}\ S_1\ \{Q_1\}, \ldots, \{P_n\}\ S_n\ \{Q_n\}$ are interference-free iff there are assertion functions pre_k and $post_k$ for $\{P_k\}\ S_k\ \{Q_k\}$ such that if T is a component of S_i and T' is an assignment or await statement in S_j $(i \neq j)$ and neither T nor T' is a proper component of an await statement, then

$$\{pre_i(T) \wedge pre_j(T')\}\ T'\ \{pre_i(T)\}$$

$$\{post_i(T) \wedge pre_j(T')\}\ T'\ \{post_i(T)\}$$

can be proved.

Just as in Chapter 2, a program proof and a pair of assertion functions are closely related.

<u>3.13. Theorem</u>: If pre and post are assertion functions for {P} S {Q} , it is possible to prove {pre(S')} S' {post(S')} for each component S' of S .

<u>Proof</u>: Same as Theorem 2.3.

<u>3.14. Theorem</u>: If there is a proof of {P} S {Q} , there are assertion functions pre and post for {P} S {Q} .

<u>Proof</u>: Same as Theorem 2.4.

<u>Examples</u>: Figure 3.2 contains a partial correctness proof for a very simple program. The fact that $\{x=0 \vee x=2\}$ S1 $\{x=1 \vee x=3\}$ and $\{x=0 \vee x=1\}$ S2 $\{x=2 \vee x=3\}$ are interference-free can be verified by four tests.

1. $\{pre(S1) \wedge pre(S2)\}$ S2 $\{pre(S1)\}$

   i.e., $\{(x=0 \vee x=2) \wedge (x=0 \vee x=1)\}$ S2 $\{x=0 \vee x=2\}$, which can be derived from $\{x=0\}$ x:=x+2 $\{x=2\}$ using A6 and A0.
2. $\{post(S1) \wedge pre(S2)\}$ S2 $\{post(S1)\}$
3. $\{pre(S2) \wedge pre(S1)\}$ S1 $\{pre(S2)\}$
4. $\{post(S2) \wedge pre(S1)\}$ S1 $\{post(S2)\}$

Note that $pre(S) \vdash (pre(S1) \wedge pre(S2))$ and $(post(S1) \wedge post(S2)) \vdash post(S)$.

```
{x=0}
S: cobegin
      {x=0 V x=2}
      S1: await true then  x:=x+1
      {x=1 V x=3}
  //
      {x=0 V x=1}
      S2: await true then  x:=x+2
      {x=2 V x=3}
   coend
{x=3}
```

Figure 3.2. A Partial Correctness Proof of a Parallel Program.

As an example of a somewhat more realistic problem, consider the program Findpos in Figure 3.3. It is essentially the same as a program whose correctness was proved by Rosen [Ro74]. Given an array x of integers, it finds the first positive component x[k] , if there is one, using two parallel processes to check the odd and even subscripted array elements. Figure 3.4 gives the assertions used in an axiomatic proof. It is not hard to see that they constitute a proof provided that the assertions for Oddsearch and Evensearch are interference-free. To verify this we must show that for each statement T in Evensearch, and each assignment T' in Oddsearch

$$\{pre(T) \land pre(T')\}\ T'\ \{pre(T)\}$$

$$\{post(T) \land pre(T')\}\ T'\ \{post(T)\}$$

(The argument that Evensearch does not interfere with Oddsearch is symmetric.) The only part of the assertions in Evensearch which could be changed by an assignment in Oddsearch is

$$i \geq \min(oddtop, eventop)$$

which might be changed when oddyes sets oddtop:=j . So we must check

$$\{i \geq \min(oddtop, eventop) \land pre(oddyes)\}\ oddtop := j$$

$$\{i \geq \min(oddtop, eventop)\}\ .$$

```
Findpos: begin integer M, x[1:M]
     initialize: i:=2; j:=1; eventop:=oddtop:=M+1;
     search: cobegin

          evensearch: while  i<min(oddtop,eventop)  do
               eventest: if  x[i]>0
                         then  evenyes:  eventop:=i
                         else  evenno:   i:=i+2
     //
          oddsearch:  while  j<min(oddtop,eventop)  do
               oddtest: if  x[j]>0
                         then  oddyes:  oddtop:=j
                         else  oddno:   j:=j+2

     coend;
     k:=min(eventop,oddtop)
end
```

Figure 3.3. The Program Findpos.

```
Findpos: begin
     initialize: i:=2; j:=1; eventop:=oddtop:=M+1;
     {i=2 Λ j=1 Λ eventop=oddtop=M+1}
     search: cobegin

          {ES}
          Evensearch: while i<min(oddtop,eventop) do
               {ES Λ i<eventop Λ i<M+1}
               eventest:  if x[i]>0
                    then  {ES Λ i<M+1 Λ x[i]>0}  evenyes: eventop:=i {ES}
                    else  {ES Λ i<eventop Λ x[i]≤0} evenno: i:=i+2   {ES}
               {ES}
          {ES Λ i≥min(oddtop,eventop)}
     //
          {OS}
          Oddsearch: while j<min(oddtop,eventop) do
                {OS Λ j<oddtop Λ j<M+1}
                oddtest:  if x[j]>0
                    then  {OS Λ j<M+1 Λ x[j]>0} oddyes: oddtop:=j     {OS}
                    else  {OS Λ j<oddtop Λ x[j]≤0} oddno: j:=j+2      {OS}
               {OS}
          {OS Λ j≥min(oddtop,eventop)}

     coend
{OS Λ ES Λ i≥min(oddtop,eventop) Λ j≥min(oddtop,eventop)}
k:=min(oddtop,eventop)
{k≤M+1 Λ ∀i(0<i<k ⇒ x[i]≤0) Λ (k≤M ⇒ x[k]>0)}
end

where  ES = {eventop≤M+1 Λ ∀k((k even Λ 0<k<i) ⇒ x[k]≤0) Λ i even
                Λ (eventop≤M ⇒ x[eventop]>0)}

       OS = {oddtop≤M+1 Λ ∀k((k odd Λ 0<k<j) ⇒ x[k]≤0) Λ j odd
                Λ (oddtop≤M ⇒ x[oddtop]>0)}
```

Figure 3.4. Partial Correctness Proof of Findpos.

Since

$$pre(oddyes) = \{OS \wedge j < oddtop \wedge x[j] > 0\}$$
$$\Rightarrow \{j < oddtop\}$$

the test is satisfied.

3.4. Consistency of the Deductive System and the Interpreter.

In Section 2.4 we discussed consistency for the two definitions of the semantics of SL. Here we derive similar results for GPL. Once again a formal proof of the main theorem is delayed until Chapter 6.

3.15. Theorem: If pre and post are assertion functions for $\{P\}\ S\ \{Q\}$, S' is a component of S, and α is a computation for S from s_0 with $P[s_0]$=true , then

1) if S' is current after α, pre(S') is true after α;
2) if α finishes S', post(S') is true after α.

Proof: By induction on the length of α. The details are given in Chapter 6. If α is empty, S is the only leaf and pre(S) is true after α since $P \vdash pre(S)$. For $\alpha = \alpha'T$, if S' is current after α, it either became current when T was executed or was already current after α'. In the first case, pre(T) is true after α' by the induction hypothesis, and starting T makes pre(S') true just as in a sequential program. In the second case, T and S' are statements from different parallel processes. By induction, pre(S') is true after α', and pre(S') remains true as T is executed because of the interference-free property.

3.16. Corollary: (Consistency for GPL) If {P} S {Q} can be proved it is true for the interpreter.

Proof: Since {P} S {Q} can be proved there are assertion functions pre and post for {P} S {Q} (Theorem 3.14). Now suppose α executes S from state s_0 with $P[s_0]$=true . Then by the last theorem, post(S)[value(s_0,α)]=true , and Q[value(s_0,α)]=true since post(S) $\vdash$ Q . So {P} S {Q} is true for the interpreter.

As a third example of a GPL proof, we consider a standard problem from the literature of parallel programming. A producer process generates a stream of values for a consumer process. Since the production and consumption of values proceeds at a variable but roughly equal pace, it is profitable to interpose a buffer between the two processes, but since storage is limited the buffer can only contain N values. Figure 3.5 shows one solution to this problem. Here the variable "in" counts the number of values which have been added to the buffer, and buffer[in mod N] is the next empty buffer position (if there is one). The variable "out" counts the number of values which have been removed, and buffer[out mod N] is the next full position. There are (in-out) values in the buffer. The <u>await</u> statement in the producer prevents a value from being added when there is no available space, while the <u>await</u> in the consumer delays removal until there is a value in the buffer to be removed.

Figure 3.6 contains a program <u>fg1</u> which computes B[k] = f(g(A[k])) , k = 1 ... M using this producer-consumer scheme. Figure 3.7a-c gives assertion functions for {M$\geq$0} fg1 {B[k]=f(g(A[k])),

```
begin comment buffer[0:N-1] is the shared buffer
              in = number of values added to buffer
              out = number of values removed from buffer
              in-out = number of elements in buffer;
   in:=out:=0;
   cobegin

       producer: . . .
                 await in-out<N then;
                 add: buffer[in mod N]:=next value;
                 markin: in:=in+1;
                 . . .
   //
       consumer: . . .
                 await in-out>0 then;
                 remove: this value := buffer[out mod N];
                 markout: out:=out+1;
                 . . .

   coend
end
```

Figure 3.5. Producer and Consumer Sharing a Bounded Buffer.

```
fgl: begin  comment  buffer[0:N-1] is the shared buffer
                     in = number of elements added to buffer
                     out = number of elements removed from buffer
                     in-out = number of elements in buffer;
      in:=out:=0;
      i:=j:=1;
      cobegin

          producer: while  i≤M  do
               begin  x:g(A[i]);
                      await in-out<N then;
                      add: buffer[in mod N]:=x;
                      markin: in:=in+1;
                      i:=i+1
               end
      //
          consumer: while  j≤M  do
               begin  await in-out>0 then;
                      remove: y:=buffer[out mod N];
                      markout: out:=out+1;
                      B[j]:=f(y);
                      j:=j+1
               end

      coend
    end
```

Figure 3.6. Computation of B[k]=f(g(A[k])), $1 \le k \le M$.

```
{M≥0}

fg1: begin

     in:=out:=0; i:=j:=1;

     {I ∧ i=in+1=1 ∧ j=out+1=1}

     cobegin

          {I ∧ i=in+1=1} producer {I}

     //

          {I ∧ j=out+1=1} consumer {I ∧ B[k]=f(g(A[k])), 1≤k≤M}

     coend

{B[k]=f(g(A[k])), 1≤k≤M}

end


I = {(buffer[(k-1) mod N]=g(A[k]),out<k≤in) ∧ 0≤in-out≤N  ∧
                           1≤i≤M+1 ∧ 1≤j≤M+1}
```

Figure 3.7a. Proof of computefg1 (main program).

```
{I ∧ i=in+1=1}

producer: while  i≤M  do

      {I ∧ i=in+1 ∧ i≤M}

      begin  x:=g(A[i]);

             {I ∧ i=in+1 ∧ i≤M ∧ x=g(A[i])}

             await in-out<N then;

             {I ∧ i=in+1 ∧ i≤M ∧ x=g(A[i]) ∧ in-out<N}

             add: buffer[in mod N]:=x;

             {I ∧ i=in+1 ∧ i≤M ∧ buffer[in mod N]=f(g(A[i])) ∧ in-out<N}

             markin: in:=in+1;

             {I ∧ i=in ∧ i≤M}

             i:=i+1;

             {I ∧ i=in+1}

      end

{I}


I = {(buffer[(k-1) mod N]=g(A[k]), out<k≤in) ∧ 0≤in-out≤N

                    ∧ 1≤i≤M+1 ∧ 1≤j≤M+1}
```

Figure 3.7b. Proof of computefgl (producer).

```
{I ∧ IC ∧ j=out+1=1}
consumer: while  j≤M  do
     {I ∧ IC ∧ j=out+1 ∧ j≤M}
      begin  await in-out>0 then;
             {I ∧ IC ∧ j=out+1 ∧ j≤M ∧ in-out>0}
             remove: y:=buffer[out mod N];
             {I ∧ IC ∧ j=out+1 ∧ j≤M ∧ y=g(A[j]) ∧ in-out>0}
             markout: out:=out+1;
             {I ∧ IC ∧ j=out ∧ j≤M ∧ y=g(A[j])}
             B[j]:=f(y);
             {I ∧ IC ∧ j=out ∧ j≤M ∧ B[j]=f(g(A[j]))}
             j:=j+1;
             {I ∧ IC ∧ j=out+1 ∧ j≤M+1}
     end
{I ∧ IC ∧ j=M+1}
{I ∧ B[k]=f(g(A[k])), 1≤k≤M}


I = {(buffer[(k-1) mod N]=g(A[k]), out<k≤in) ∧ 0≤in-out≤N
                     ∧ 1≤i≤M+1 ∧ 1≤j≤M+1}


IC = {B[k]=f(g(A[k])), 1≤k<j}
```

Figure 3.7c. Proof of computefg1 (consumer).

$1 \leq k \leq M\}$. The reader can verify that the assertions satisfy Definition 3.11. To satisfy the interference-free criteria, assertions in the consumer must be invariant over statements in the producer and vice versa. Consider the form of the assertions in the consumer. Each consists of the invariant I plus some relations between variables which are not changed in the producer. In addition, two assertions contain the clause (in-out > 0). The assignments in the producer leave these three components unchanged: I is also an invariant in the producer; the variables in the second component are not affected; and the only assignment that changes (in-out) is markin: in:=in+1 which leaves (in-out > 0) true. Similar reasoning shows that assertions in the producer are invariant over statements in the consumer, so the interference-free criterion is satisfied.

3.5. Auxiliary Variables.

In many cases the axioms and inference rules A0-A7 are not strong enough to prove a partial correctness formula which is true. Figure 3.8 is an example of a program where the deductive system fails. The formula {x=0} add1 {x=2} is true, but it can't be proved using A0-A7. To see this, consider post(adda). If the program starts with x=0 , it can finish adda with x=1 or x=2 , depending on whether or not addb has been executed. So the strongest possible assertion for post(adda) is {x=1 V x=2} . The same is true for post(addb). Since (post(adda) Λ post(addb)) $\vdash$ post(add1) , the strongest possible assertion for post(add1) is (x=1 V x=2) , in spite of the fact that after executing add1, x must have the value 2.

```
{x=0}

add1: cobegin

          {x=0 V x=1}

          adda: await true then  x:=x+1

          {x=1 V x=2}

      //

          {x=0 V x=1}

          addb: await true then  x:=x+1

          {x=1 V x=2}

      coend

{x=1 V x=2}
```

Figure 3.8. The Program add1.

Now consider Figure 3.9, an expanded version of add1. The reader can verify that the assertions in Figure 3.9 are interference-free and yield a proof of {x=0} add2 {x=2} . The proof depends on the variables y and z . Since add2 has the same effect on x as add1, we would like to be able to conclude from this that {x=0} add1 {x=2} . In order to do this we will define the concept of auxiliary variables and then give a new inference rule to allow their use.

The program add2 has essentially the same behavior as add1, in spite of the fact that it contains statements and variables which do not appear in add1. This is because the additional variables, and the statements using them, do not affect the flow of control or the values assigned to x . Variables which are used in this way in a program will be called <u>auxiliary variables</u>. The need for auxiliary variables in proofs of parallel programs has also been recognized by Brinch Hansen [Br73] and Lauer [La73].

<u>3.17. Definition</u>: Let AV be a set of variables which appear in S only in assignment statements

x:=E where $x \in AV$, and any variables may be used in E .

Then AV is an auxiliary variable set for S .

<u>3.18. Definition</u>: Let AV be an auxiliary variable set for S . S is a <u>reduction</u> of S' with respect to AV iff S can be obtained from S' by one of the following operations.

```
{x=0}
add2: begin
        {x=0}
        y:=0; z:=0;
        {x=y=z=0}
        cobegin
              {x=z ∧ y=0}
              await true then begin x:=x+1; y:=1 end
              {x=z+1 ∧ y=1}
        //
              {x=y ∧ z=0}
              await true then begin x:=x+1; z:=1  end
              {x=y+1 ∧ z=1}
        coend
{(x=z+1 ∧ y=1) ∧ (x=y+1 ∧ z=1)}
end
{x=2}
```

Figure 3.9. The Program add2.

1. Deleting x:=E , where x ε AV
2. Replacing <u>await</u> true <u>then</u> x:=E by x:=E , provided x:=E makes at most one reference to a shared variable. (In this case, x does not have to be an element of AV.)
3. Replacing <u>begin</u> S <u>end</u> by S .

We will write S=reduce(S',S_0) , where S_0 is the statement eliminated in going from S' to S , i.e., in 1) S_0 is the assignment, in 2) the <u>await</u> statement, and in 3) the <u>begin</u> - <u>end</u>.

In our example, add1 can be obtained from add2 by repeated applications of the operations above. Note that in order to reduce <u>await</u> true <u>then</u> <u>begin</u> x:=x+1; y:=1 <u>end</u> to <u>await</u> true <u>then</u> x:=x+1 we must first delete y:=1 (operation 1), then the <u>begin</u> - <u>end</u> brackets (operation 3). The synchronization statement cannot be removed because x:=x+1 contains two references to x . It is safe to remove a synchronization statement when rule 2 applies, because then the assignment statement can be treated as indivisible anyway.

Now we give the inference rule which allows us to conclude {x=0} add1 {x=2} from a proof of {x=0} add2 {x=2} .

<u>A8 Auxiliary Variables.</u>

If AV is an auxiliary variable set for S' , S a reduction of S' with respect to AV, and P and Q assertions which do not contain free any variables from AV, then

$$\frac{\{P\}\ S'\ \{Q\}}{\{P\}\ S\ \{Q\}}$$

In order to establish that this inference rule is consistent with the interpreter, we must show that if {P} S' {Q} is true for the interpreter, {P} S {Q} is too. To do this we will show that there is a relationship between the computations of S and S' .

3.19. Lemma: Suppose S=reduce(S',S_0) is a reduction of S' with respect to AV, and α is a computation for S . Then $\exists\alpha'$, a computation for S' , such that

1) $x[\text{value}(s_0,\alpha')] = x[\text{value}(s_0,\alpha)]$ for $x \notin AV$
2) if reduce(T,S_0) is current after α , T is current after α' , where T is any component of S' .

Proof: Let α' be like α except that S_0 is executed in α' as soon as it is ready to be executed. The only difference between α and α' is that α' may contain occurrences of S_0 . S_0 may change the value of a variable in AV, but it has no effect on other values. The variables in AV do not affect the flow of control, since they do not appear in the conditions of if, while or await statements. Thus, the flow of control is the same in S and S' , and α' is a computation for S' for which 1) and 2) above are true.

3.20 Theorem: If {P} S' {Q} is true for the interpreter and the requirements of A8 are satisfied, {P} S {Q} is true for the interpreter.

Proof: Let α be a computation for S with $P[s_0]$=true . Let α' be the computation for S' from Lemma 3.19. Since {P} S' {Q} is true in the model, $Q[\text{value}(s_0,\alpha')]$=true . Then $Q[\text{value}(s_0,\alpha)]$=true , since Q has no variables from AV. Thus, {P} S {Q} is true in the model.

Auxiliary variables can be a very powerful aid in program proofs. Starting with a program such as add1, new variables and statements can be added to yield a program like add2 for which a proof is possible. Then A8 can be applied repeatedly to give a proof for the original program. If the new statements obey the following restrictions, it will always be possible to remove them again using A8.

1. assignments must be to the new variables.
2. synchronization statements must contain at most one statement (and that must be an assignment) from the original program.
3. <u>begin</u> - <u>end</u> may be used freely as long as the result is syntactically correct.
4. no other kind of statement is added.

As another example of the use of auxiliary variables, consider a second version of the producer and consumer program of Figure 3.6. The program fg2 in Figure 3.10 uses semaphores "full" and "empty" to synchronize access to the buffer. Figure 3.11 shows the translation of the semaphore operations into GPL (as defined in Section 3.1), and includes auxiliary variables Pempty, Vempty, Pfull, Vfull. Figure 3.12a and 3.12b gives assertion functions for $\{M\geq 0\}$ fg2' $\{B[k]=f(g(A[k])), 1\leq k\leq M\}$ (the producer is omitted, but it is similar to the consumer). The reader can verify that these assertions satisfy Definition 3.11; the proof is essentially the same as for the earlier version of the producer and consumer. Using A8, the auxiliary variables can be removed to yield a proof of $\{M\geq 0\}$ fg2 $\{B[k]=f(g(A[k])), 1\leq k\leq M\}$. Habermann [Ha72] presents this solution to the producer-

```
fg2: begin  comment buffer[0:N-1] is the shared buffer
                    full = number of full places in buffer (semaphore)
                    empty = number of empty places in buffer (semaphore);
    full:=0; empty:=N; i:=j:=1;
    cobegin
        producer: while  i≤M  do
            begin  x:=g(A[i]);
                   P(empty);
                   buffer[i mod N]:=x;
                   V(full);
                   i:=i+1;
            end
    //
        consumer: while  j≤M  do
            begin  P(full);
                   y:=buffer[j mod N];
                   V(empty);
                   B[j]:=f(y);
                   j:=j+1;
            end
    coend
end
```

Figure 3.10. A Second Version of the Producer-Consumer Program.

```
fg2': begin comment  Pempty, Vempty, Pfull, Vfull are auxiliary variables;
    full:=0; empty:=N; i:=j:=1;
    Pfull:=Vfull:=Pempty:=Vempty:=0;
    cobegin
          producer: while  i≤M  do
             begin  x:=g(A[i]);
                    await empty>0 then
                       begin empty:=empty-1; Pempty:=Pempty+1  end
                    buffer[i mod N]:=x;
                    await true then
                       begin full:=full+1; Vfull:=Vfull+1  end
                    i:=i+1;
             end
    //
          consumer: while  j≤M  do
             begin  await full>0 then
                       begin full:=full-1; Pfull:=Pfull+1  end
                    y:=buffer[j mod N];
                    await true then
                       begin empty:=empty+1; Vempty:=Vempty+1  end
                    B[j]:=f(y);
                   j:=j+1;
             end
    coend
end
```

Figure 3.11. Program fg2': A Translation of fg2 into GPL.

```
{M≥0}
fg2': begin
      full:=0; empty:=N; i:=j:=1;
      Pfull:=Vfull:=Pempty:=Vempty:=0;
      {I ∧ Vfull=Pempty ∧ i=Vfull+1=1 ∧ Vempty=Pfull ∧ j=Vempty+1=1}
      cobegin

            {I ∧ Vfull=Pempty ∧ i=Vfull+1=1}
            producer
            {I}

      //

            {I ∧ Vempty=Pfull ∧ j=Vempty+1=1}
            consumer
            {I ∧ B[k]=f(g(A[k])), 1≤k≤M}

      coend
end
{B[k]=f(g(A[k])), 1≤k≤M}


I = {(buffer[k mod N]=g(A[k]), Vempty<k≤Vfull) ∧ full=Vfull-Pfull
                 ∧ empty=N+Vempty-Pempty ∧ 1≤i≤M+1 ∧ 1≤j≤M+1}
```

Figure 3.12a. Proof of fg2' (main program).

```
{I ∧ IC ∧ Vempty=Pfull ∧ j=Vempty+1=1}
consumer: while  j≤M  do
    {I ∧ IC ∧ j≤M ∧ Vempty=Pfull ∧ j=Vempty+1}
    begin  await full>0 then
              begin full:=full-1; Pfull:=Pfull+1 end;
           {I ∧ IC ∧ j≤M ∧ Vempty=Pfull-1 ∧ j=Vempty+1 ∧ Vfull-Vempty>0}
           y:=buffer[j mod N];
           {I ∧ IC ∧ j≤M ∧ Vempty=Pfull-1 ∧ j=Vempty+1 ∧ y=g(A[j])}
           await true then
              begin empty:=empty+1; Vempty:=Vempty+1 end;
           {I ∧ IC ∧ j≤M ∧ Vempty=Pfull ∧ j=Vempty ∧ y=g(A[j])}
           B[j]:=f(y);
           {I ∧ IC ∧ j≤M ∧ Vempty=Pfull ∧ j=Vempty ∧ B[j]=f(g(A[j]))}
           j:=j+1;
           {I ∧ IC ∧ j≤M+1 ∧ Vempty=Pfull ∧ j=Vempty+1}
    end
{I ∧ IC ∧ j=M+1} ⇒ {B[k]=f(g(A[k])), 1≤k≤M}


I = {(buffer[k mod N]=g(A[k]), Vempty<k≤Vfull) ∧ full=Vfull-Pfull
                ∧ empty=N+Vempty-Pempty ∧ 1≤i≤M+1 ∧ 1<j≤M+1}


IC = {B[k]=f(g(A[k])), 1≤k<j}
```

Figure 3.12b. Proof of fg2' (consumer).

consumer problem and provides an informal proof of its correctness. For the proof he uses special functions which count the number of P and V operations on each semaphore; these play the same role as our auxiliary variables.

3.6. Mutual Exclusion.

It is often necessary to ensure that certain critical sections in separate processes cannot be executed at the same time. Most often this is because the critical sections manipulate shared variables, and it is essential to prevent them from interfering with each other. One of the standard ways of ensuring mutual exclusion is the use of a semaphore mutex, whose initial value is 1. Each process executes P(mutex) on entering its critical section and V(mutex) on leaving. Our techniques can be used to show that this discipline does indeed ensure mutual exclusion as long as there are no other operations on the semaphore mutex.

Figure 3.13 shows a group of cyclic processes containing critical sections. The statements in the critical and noncritical sections are not specified, but they do not operate on mutex. In Section 3.1 we suggested a representation of the P and V operations as

P(sem) = <u>await</u> sem>0 <u>then</u> sem:=sem-1

V(sem) = <u>await</u> true <u>then</u> sem:=sem+1

Thus, the code for implementing mutual exclusion in GPL is

```
begin
    mutex:=1;
    cobegin  S1  //
             . . .
             // Si: while true do
                    begin noncritical part;
                          P(mutex);
                          critical section i;
                          V(mutex);
                          noncritical part;
                    end
             . . .
             // Sn
    coend
end
```

mutex is not changed in the critical and noncritical sections

Figure 3.13. Critical Sections with Mutual Exclusion.

```
await  mutex>0  then  mutex:=mutex-1 ;
critical section  i ;
await true then  mutex:=mutex+1 ;
```

In order to prove that this accomplishes mutual exclusion we will use an array of auxiliary variables inCS[1:n] . Initially, inCS[i]=0, $1 \leq i \leq n$, and it will be manipulated on entering and leaving critical sections.

```
await  mutex>0  then begin  mutex:=mutex-1 ;
                            inCS[i]:=1
                      end
critical section  i ;
await true then begin  mutex:=mutex+1 ;
                       inCS[i]:=0
                 end
```

Figure 3.14 shows the program of Figure 3.13 with the auxiliary variables. The assertion that inCS[i]=0 on reaching the critical section code and 1 throughout the critical section is justified because there are no other operations on inCS[i] . Similarly the assertion that I holds at all times assumes that there are no other operations on mutex. The interference-free requirement for assertions in process i is easily verified, because each assertion is a statement about inCS[i] , which is not changed in S_j if $i \neq j$, and I, which is invariant over the statements in process j .

Now suppose that there is some computation α in which S_i and S_j , $i \neq j$, are executing their critical sections at the same time.

```
{true}
begin  mutex:=1; inCS:=0;
    {I ∧ inCS[i]=0, i=1,...,n}
    cobegin  S1 //...// Sn  coend
    {false}
end
{false}

    {I ∧ inCS[i]=0}
    Si: while true do
        begin {I ∧ inCS[i]=0}
              noncritical section;
              {I ∧ inCS[i]=0}
              await mutex>0 then begin mutex:=mutex-1; inCS[i]:=1 end;
              {I ∧ inCS[i]=1}
              critical section i;
              {I ∧ inCS[i]=1}
              await true then begin mutex:=mutex+1; inCS[i]:=0 end;
              {I ∧ inCS[i]=0}
              noncritical section;
              {I ∧ inCS[i]=0}
        end
    {false}
```

$$I = \{mutex=(1 - \sum_{k=1}^{n} inCS[k]) \land mutex \geq 0 \land \forall j(inCS[j]=0 \text{ or } 1)\}$$

mutex and inCS are not changed in the critical and noncritical sections

Figure 3.14. Mutual Exclusion Program with Auxiliary Variables.

Since $\{inCS[k]=1 \wedge I\}$ is true throughout the critical section in process k , $(inCS[i]=1 \wedge inCS[j]=1 \wedge I)$ is true after α . But $(inCS[i]=1 \wedge inCS[j]=1 \wedge I) \Rightarrow mutex<0 \wedge mutex \geq 0 \Rightarrow false$. So no such α exists.

Proofs of mutual exclusion will be discussed more extensively in Chapter 5. For now we close by giving an example of the use of mutual exclusion in a proof of partial correctness. Figure 3.15 is a rewriting of the program add1 of Figure 3.8. Here, instead of representing x:=x+1 as an indivisible statement, it is written as a:=x ; x:=a+1 , where a is a local variable. Semaphores are used to guarantee mutual exclusion for the critical sections which operate on x . Figure 3.16 is an extension of this program, using auxiliary variables. The proof of the interference-free property for the two parallel statements makes use of mutual exclusion. For example, to show that pre(add1) = $\{x=a=z \wedge y=0 \wedge inCS[1]=1 \wedge I\}$ is invariant over add2 we must prove

$$\{pre(add1) \wedge pre(add2)\}\ add2\ \{pre(add1)\}\ .$$

But pre(add1) $\wedge$ pre(add2) $\Rightarrow$ false , so this is the same as proving

$$\{false\}\ add2\ \{pre(add1)\}\ .$$

Now {false} S {false} can be proved for any statement S , as can be shown by induction on the structure of S . Since false $\vdash$ P for any assertion P , {false} S {P} can also be proved. So in particular we can prove {false} add2 {pre(add1)} . In general, an assertion P

```
add3: begin
      mutex:=1;
      cobegin
           S1: begin  P(mutex);
                      a:=x;
                      x:=a+1;
                      V(mutex);
               end
      //
           S2: begin  P(mutex);
                      b:=x;
                      x:=b+1;
                      V(mutex);
               end
      coend
end
```

Figure 3.15. The Program add3.

```
{x=0}
add4: begin  y:=z:=0; mutex:=1; inCS[1]:=inCS[2]:=0;
             {x=y=z=0 ∧ inCS[1]=inCS[2]=0 ∧ I}
             cobegin  S1 // S2  coend
             {x=2}
      end
{x=2}

S1: {x=z ∧ y=0 ∧ inCS[1]=0 ∧ I}
    begin  {x=z ∧ y=0 ∧ inCS[1]=0 ∧ I}
           await mutex>0 then begin mutex:=mutex-1; inCS[1]:=1  end
           {x=z ∧ y=0 ∧ inCS[1]=1 ∧ I}
           a:=x;
           {x=a=z ∧ y=0 ∧ inCS[1]=1 ∧ I}
           add1: x:=a+1;
           {x=z+1 ∧ y=0 ∧ inCS[1]=1 ∧ I}
           y:=1;
           {x=z+1 ∧ y=1 ∧ inCS[1]=1 ∧ I}
           await true then begin mutex:=mutex+1; inCS[1]=0  end
           {x=z+1 ∧ y=1 ∧ inCS[1]=0 ∧ I}
    end
{x=z+1 ∧ y=1 ∧ inCS[1]=0 ∧ I}

S2 is symmetric: {x=y ∧ z=0 ∧ inCS[2]=0 ∧ I} S2 {x=y+1 ∧ z=1 ∧ inCS[2]=0 ∧ I}
```

$$I = \{mutex=(1 - \sum_{k=1}^{2} inCS[k]) \wedge mutex \geq 0 \wedge inCS[k]=0 \text{ or } 1\}$$

Figure 3.16. The Program add4.

in a critical section is invariant over assignments in other critical sections because the invariance test reduces to {false} S {P} .

Program add4 has auxiliary variables y and inCS . The statements which manipulate these variables can be removed using A8, giving a proof of {x=0} add3 {x=2} .

We have only sketched the proof for program add4; a complete presentation would require verifying that every assignment and await in S1 preserved every assertion in S2, and vice versa. Even for such a small program this would be a large task, and it is a task which grows exponentially in the size of the program. Thus, proofs for GPL programs quickly become unmanageable. In the next chapter we will introduce a parallel programming language in which mutual exclusion is provided syntactically. This removes much of the complexity in the interactions between processes and greatly simplifies the process of proving that a program is correct.

CHAPTER 4

THE RESTRICTED PARALLEL LANGUAGE (RPL)

The programming language presented in this chapter is essentially a restricted version of the general parallel language of Chapter 3. The powerful await statement is replaced by another, more limited, synchronizing statement called withwhen. The use of shared variables is governed by strict syntactic requirements which guarantee that only one process at a time has access to a given variable. Since much of the complexity of parallel program behavior is due to interference between processes accessing a common variable, the result of these restrictions is that RPL programs are more intellectually manageable than programs written in GPL. They are also much easier to prove correct. The proof of a program in GPL requires that parallel processes satisfy the interference-free property; verifying this is in general an n-squared problem. The corresponding property for RPL programs, called "Einmischungsfrei", can be verified in linear time. This saving is accomplished by restricting both the syntax of the language and the assertions in the proof. It is similar to the simplification of proofs when the undisciplined use of go to statements is eliminated.

RPL is based on a parallel language defined by Hoare [Ho72] and is similar to one proposed by Brinch Hansen [Br72a]. Hoare gave a set of axioms and inference rules for his language, however they were not strong enough to provide proofs in a number of cases. The proof rules A0-A7 in Table 4.1 are derived from Hoare's, but are stronger.

Together with A8, they form a "complete" deductive system for the partial correctness of parallel programs in RPL, as will be shown in Chapter 6.

Section 4.1 defines the syntax of RPL, and 4.2 and 4.3 give its semantics in terms of an interpretive model and axioms. Section 4.4 shows that the interpreter and the axioms are consistent. Much of this work makes use of results derived in Chapter 3.

4.1. The Language.

RPL is defined by adding two statements to the sequential language of Chapter 2. Parallel execution is initiated by the statement

<u>resource</u> r_1(variable list),...,r_m(variable list):

<u>cobegin</u> S_1//...//S_n <u>coend</u>

Here the resources $r_1 \ldots r_m$ are groups of shared variables, and the S_i are statements to be executed in parallel. Again, no assumption is made about the way parallelism is implemented, or about the relative speeds of the S_i. It is legitimate to nest one parallel statement inside another. The only restriction is that the resources in the two statements be distinct.

<u>4.1. Definition</u>: Components T_1 and T_2 of S are in <u>different processes</u> of S iff S contains a statement

<u>resource</u> $r_1,\ldots,r_m$: <u>cobegin</u> S_1//...//S_n <u>coend</u>

with T_1 and T_2 components of different S_i . Otherwise, T_1 and T_2 are in the same process.

The second new statement provides for synchronization and protection of shared variables.

with r when B do S

has the following interpretation: r is a resource, B is a Boolean expression, and S is a statement which uses the variables of r . S is called the critical section of the withwhen statement. Execution of a critical section can only begin when B is true, and while it is being executed no other process can execute a critical section for the same resource. If several processes are competing for a resource r , we make no assumptions about the order in which they receive it. The statement with r when true do S can be abbreviated as with r do S .

It is possible to implement the statement with r when B do S using the GPL await statement. One method is

```
begin  await  B ∧ ¬busyr  then  busyr:=true ;
       S;
       await true then  busyr:=false
end
```

where busyr is a new variable which is initialized with the value false. For a discussion of the implementation of withwhen using standard synchronizing operations see Hoare [Ho72] and Sintzoff and van Lamsweerde [Si75].

Withwhen statements can only be used inside cobegin statements, and withwhen statements for the same resource cannot be nested.

In order to guarantee that operations on shared variables are well-defined, the syntax of the language restricts the way variables are used in parallel processes.

4.2. Definition: Let S be the parallel statement

$$\underline{\text{resource}}\ r_1,\ldots,r_m\text{: }\underline{\text{cobegin}}\ S_1//\ldots//S_n\ \underline{\text{coend}}$$

Then $Var(S)$ = the set of variables used in S

$R(S) = \{x\text{: } x \in r_i \vee x$ is in a resource r declared in a parallel statement containing S, with S not a component of a critical section for $r\}$

$R(S)$ is called the resource variables of S.

$V_k(S) = \{x\text{: } x \in Var(S)$ and no statement of S_j, $j \neq k$ assigns a value to $x\}$

$V_k(S)$ is called the local variables of S_k.

Note that the resource variables of S are those variables which must be protected by critical sections when they are used inside S. In addition to the variables from $r_1 \ldots r_m$, they include variables from resources declared in parallel statements which contain S. The syntactic restrictions on variables are expressed in terms of these classes.

4.3. Definition: A parallel statement in RPL must obey the following restrictions:

1) $Var(S) = R(S) \cup V_1(S) \cup \ldots \cup V_n(S)$;
2) No variable belongs to more than one resource;
3) If $x \in R(S)$, x appears in S_k only in a withwhen statement for the resource containing x .
4) If x appears in S_k , x is either a local variable for S_k or a resource variable.

These requirements can easily be checked at compile time. Their purpose is to guarantee that two processes cannot interfere with each other by simultaneously operating on any variable. Rule 1 requires that every variable is a resource variable or is local to some process S_k , or both. If it is a resource variable, it belongs to exactly one resource r (rule 2), and is accessible only in a withwhen statement for r (rule 3), which prevents two processes from using it simultaneously. If it is a local variable for S_k it is not changed in any S_i if $i \neq k$, so the reference in S_k is unambiguous. If a variable is local to more than one process, it is not changed by any of them, so there is no conflict even if two processes access it simultaneously.

In GPL it was necessary to limit the form of statements which referred to shared variables. For example, x:=x+1 was not a legitimate statement if x appeared in more than one process. These restrictions were required to ensure that the interpreter accurately modelled parallel execution. In RPL these problems do not arise, since references to shared variables are allowed only in critical sections, and only one process at a time can execute a critical section for a given resource. Statements like x:=x+1 are acceptable, even if x is a shared variable.

Example 1: Add5 (Figure 4.1) is another version of the program of Figure 3.8. Here withwhen statements are used to control access to the shared variable x .

Example 2: Producer and Consumer sharing a bounded buffer.

Figure 4.2 shows a third solution (due to Hoare [Ho72]) for the producer and consumer problem introduced in Chapter 3. Note the similarity to the solution in Figure 3.5. The critical section in the producer can only be started when there is free space in the buffer (count<N), and the critical section in the consumer can only be started when the buffer is not empty (count>0).

4.2. The Interpretive Model.

The interpreter for RPL programs is very much like the one defined in Chapter 3 for GPL programs. The program state remains the same, and the state transition function "next" is extended to cover withwhen statements. This requires a definition of the states in which a withwhen statement is ready to be executed.

4.4. Definition: A statement S is current in the program state s=(c,v) iff S is a leaf in c .

```
add5: resource rx(x): cobegin
        adda: with rx do x:=x+1;
  //
        addb: with rx do x:=x+1;
  coend
```

Figure 4.1. Program add5.

```
begin
    comment inpointer = position of next empty space in buffer
            outpointer = position of next full space in buffer
            count = number of elements in buffer;
    count:=inpointer:=outpointer:=0;
    parallel: resource Bufman(inpointer,outpointer,count,buffer[0:N-1]):
      cobegin
        producer: . . .
            add: with Bufman when count<N do
                 begin  inpointer:=(inpointer+1) mod N;
                        buffer[inpointer]:=next value;
                        count:=count+1
                 end
            . . .
      //
        consumer: . . .
            remove: with Bufman when count>0 do
                 begin  outpointer:=(outpointer+1) mod N;
                        this value:=buffer[outpointer];
                        count:=count-1
                 end
            . . .
      coend
end
```

Figure 4.2. Producer and Consumer Using a Bounded Buffer.

4.5. Definition: A resource r is busy in program state s iff a proper component of a withwhen statement which uses r is current in s (i.e., iff a critical section for r is in execution in s).

4.6. Definition: A statement S is ready to execute in the program state s iff

1) S is current in s , and
2) if S is with r when B do S_1 , B[s]=true and r is not busy in s .

4.7. Definition: The state transition function next: {program states} × {statements} → {program states} is given by

next((c,v),S) = undefined if S is not ready to execute in (c,v)
= (c',v) where c' = replace(c,S,S_1) , if S = with r when B do S_1
= (c',v') of Definition 3.4 otherwise.

Note that with r when B do S is not ready to execute if a critical section for r is already in execution, so only one process at a time can execute a critical section for r .

The concepts of a computation, and of finishing or executing a statement, are defined in much the same way as in Chapter 3.

4.8. Definition: A computation α for program S beginning with variable state v_0 is a sequence of statements $S_1 \ldots S_n$ such that if $s_0 = (S,v_0)$, the sequence of states $s_i = next(s_{i-1},S_i)$, $i=1 \ldots n$ is defined, i.e., S_i is ready to execute after $S_1 \ldots S_{i-1}$. In this case <u>value</u>$(s_0,\alpha)=s_n$.

4.9. Definition: If α is a computation for S , and S' is a component of S , α finishes S' iff

S' is assign, null, while, begin ... end, if or cobegin ... coend -- same as Definition 3.7.

S' is with r when B do S_1 and α finishes S_1 .

4.10. Definition: $\{P\}\ S\ \{Q\}$ is true in the interpretive model iff any computation α which executes S from an initial state s_0 in which P is true has $Q[value(s_0,\alpha)]=true$.

In Chapters 5 and 6 we will need to know some properties of computations and resources. The following lemma is the basis for this work. It states that if a resource r is busy for a computation α , it must be busy because some process has started a withwhen statement S_1 for r and has not yet finished it. From the time that S_1 was started in α , no other process can have access to r .

4.11. Lemma: r is busy for α iff α can be written $\alpha = \alpha_0\ S_1\ \alpha_1 \ldots S_k\ \alpha_k$, where

1) S_1 is with r when B do S' , and S' is in execution for α ;
2) $S_1,\ldots,S_k$ are from the same process;
3) none of the statements in $\alpha_1,\ldots,\alpha_k$ are from the same process as S_1 ;

4) If T is in α_i ($i \geq 1$) the variables in r are not referenced in T .

Proof: r is busy for α iff a critical section which uses r is in execution, and this can only happen if a withwhen statement appears in α and is not finished by α . Then α can be written in the form above, satisfying 1-3. To see that 4 is also satisfied, recall the syntactic restrictions of Definition 4.3. If T uses a variable from r , T must be a component of a withwhen statement for r . But then if T appears in α_i , two critical sections for r are in execution at the same time, and this is not possible.

4.3. Axioms and Inference Rules.

Table 4.1 gives the axioms and inference rules for the restricted parallel language. They are similar to the axioms for parallel programs given by Hoare [Ho72]. However, Hoare does not provide for auxiliary variables, and his version of A7 is more restricted in the variables which can be used in assertions. A0-A5 and A8 are the same as the corresponding rules in Chapter 3, while A6 and A7 give the semantics of the two new statements. Both rules use the resource invariant $I(r)$, an assertion which describes the acceptable states of the variables in resource r . A7 includes the provision that the proof of $\{P_i\}\ S_i\ \{Q_i\}$ be Einmischungsfrei. This condition is related to the interference-free requirement for GPL programs, but it is more easily verified. It requires that the variables used in each line

A0 consequence

$$\frac{\{P'\}\ S\ \{Q'\}\ ,\quad P \vdash P'\ ,\quad Q' \vdash Q}{\{P\}\ S\ \{Q\}}$$

A1 assignment

$$\{P^x_E\}\ x{:=}E\ \{P\}$$

A2 null

$$\{P\}\ ;\ \{P\}$$

A3 composition

$$\frac{\{P_1\}\ S_1\ \{P_2\}\ ,\quad \{P_2\}\ S_2\ \{P_3\},\ldots,\{P_n\}\ S_n\ \{P_{n+1}\}}{\{P_1\}\ \underline{\text{begin}}\ S_1;\ldots;S_n\ \underline{\text{end}}\ \{P_{n+1}\}}$$

A4 alternation

$$\frac{\{P \wedge B\}\ S_1\ \{Q\}\ ,\quad \{P \wedge \neg B\}\ S_2\ \{Q\}}{\{P\}\ \underline{\text{if}}\ B\ \underline{\text{then}}\ S_1\ \underline{\text{else}}\ S_2\ \{Q\}}$$

A5 iteration

$$\frac{\{P \wedge B\}\ S\ \{P\}}{\{P\}\ \underline{\text{while}}\ B\ \underline{\text{do}}\ S\ \{P \wedge \neg B\}}$$

A6 critical section

$$\frac{\{P \wedge B \wedge I(r)\}\ S\ \{Q \wedge I(r)\}}{\{P\}\ \underline{\text{with}}\ r\ \underline{\text{when}}\ B\ \underline{\text{do}}\ S\ \{Q\}}$$

A7 parallel

$$\frac{\{P_i\}\ S_i\ \{Q_i\}\ \text{is Einmischungsfrei},\ 1 \le i \le n}{\begin{array}{l}\{P_1 \wedge\ldots\wedge P_n \wedge I(r_1) \wedge\ldots\wedge I(r_m)\}\\ \quad \underline{\text{resource}}\ r_1(\ ),\ldots,r_m(\ ):\ \underline{\text{cobegin}}\ S_1//\ldots//S_n\ \underline{\text{coend}}\\ \{Q_1 \wedge\ldots\wedge Q_n \wedge I(r_1) \wedge\ldots\wedge I(r_m)\}\end{array}}$$

A8 auxiliary variables

If AV is an auxiliary variable set for S', S a reduction of S' with respect to AV, and P and Q assertions which do not contain free any variables from AV $\dfrac{\{P\}\ S'\ \{Q\}}{\{P\}\ S\ \{Q\}}$

Table 4.1. Axioms and Inference Rules for the Restricted Parallel Language.

$\{P'\}\ S'\ \{Q'\}$ of the proof of $\{P_i\}\ S_i\ \{Q_i\}$ be only those variables which process S_i has a right to access at S'. These are, roughly, the local variables of S_i, plus the variables for resource r if S is a component of a critical section for r. For a precise definition of Einmischungsfrei, we need the concept of the <u>proof-variables</u> of a statement or resource.

<u>4.12. Definition</u>: Let S' be a statement and r a resource in program S, with r declared in the parallel statement T, and let T' be the statement which immediately contains S'. Then

Proof-var(r) = {x: x is not assigned a value in T except in a critical section for r}

Proof-var(S') = variables of S, if S'=S

= $V_k(T') \cap$ Proof-var(T') is S' is the kth process in parallel statement T'

= Proof-var(T') $\cup$ Proof-var(r), if T' is <u>with</u> r <u>when</u> B <u>do</u> S'

= Proof-var(T') otherwise.

Note that Proof-var(r) includes all the variables which belong to resource r, and may also contain other variables. The variables in Proof-var(S') are either local to the process containing S' or belong to Proof-var(r), where S' is a component of a critical section for r.

<u>4.13. Definition</u>: Suppose S is the parallel statement

<u>resource</u> $r_1,\ldots,r_m$: <u>cobegin</u> $S_1//\ldots//S_n$ <u>coend</u>

Then {P} S {Q} is Einmischungsfrei iff it has a proof in which

1) all free variables in $I(r_j)$ are elements of Proof-var(r_j), $1 \leq j \leq m$

2) if S' is a component of S, and {P'} S' {Q'} is a line in the proof, then all free variables in P' and Q' are in Proof-var(S').

The variables in Proof-var(S') are exactly those which cannot be changed by another process when pre(S') and post(S') are expected to hold, i.e., when S' is ready to execute or has finished.

4.14. Lemma: Let S and T be statements in different processes of a program S', and α be a computation for S'. Suppose S is current after α, or α finishes S. Then, if T is ready to execute after α, T does not change a variable in Proof-var(S).

Proof: Since S and T are in different processes of S', there is a statement T'=resource $r_1,\ldots,r_m$: cobegin $T_1//\ldots//T_n$ coend with S a component of T_i and T a component of T_j, $i \neq j$. Suppose T changes variable x. Then $x \notin V_i(T')$, so if $x \in$ Proof-var(S) it must belong to a resource r, with S a proper component of a withwhen statement S_1 for r. T must also be a proper component of a withwhen S_2 for r, because of the syntactic restrictions of RPL. $S_1 \neq S_2$, since they are in different processes, and both are in execution for α. This is not possible, so $x \notin$ Proof-var(S).

Rules A6 and A7 are presented in a way which makes it easy to produce proofs which are Einmischungsfrei. The pre- and post- assertions of the parallel statement will usually contain an assertion about the local variables of each process (V_k) and an assertion about each resource. The resource invariant holds when parallel execution begins, and is preserved by each critical section. Since its variables are only modified inside critical sections, this means that the invariant holds whenever no critical section is in execution; in particular it holds when parallel execution ends.

Inference rule A6 reflects the fact that a process may assume that the invariant holds when it gains access to the resource, but that nothing else is known about the shared variables. When the process leaves the critical section it cannot make any assumptions about the state of the resource, since that may be changed unpredictably by another process.

Example 1: Figure 4.3 gives an informal proof of the program add6, which is obtained from add5 by inserting an auxiliary variable y[1:2]. The program variables are x and y, and the variable classes of Definitions 4.2 and 4.12 are:

Var(par) = {x,y}	
R(par) = {x}	Proof-var(rx) = {x,y[1],y[2]}
V_1(par) = {y[1]}	Proof-var(adda) = {y[1]}
V_2(par) = {y[2]}	Proof-var(addb) = {y[2]}

The reader can verify that the proof is Einmischungsfrei. Repeated application of A8 gives a proof of {x=0} add5 {x=2}.

```
{x=0}
begin comment  y[1], y[2] are auxiliary variables;
    y[1]:=y[2]:=0;
    {y[1]=0 ∧ y[2]=0 ∧ I(rx)}
    par: resource rx(x): cobegin
        {y[1]=0}
        adda: with rx do
            {y[1]=0 ∧ I(rx)}
            begin  x:=x+1; y[1]:=1  end
            {y[1]=1 ∧ I(rx)}
        {y[1]=1}
    //
        {y[2]=0}
        addb: with rx do
            {y[2]=0 ∧ I(rx)}
            begin  x:=x+1; y[2]:=1  end
            {y[2]=1 ∧ I(rx)}
        {y[2]=1}
    coend
    {y[1]=1 ∧ y[2]=1 ∧ I(rx)}
end
{x=2}

I(rx) = {x = y[1] + y[2]}
```

Figure 4.3. An Informal Proof of {x=0} add6 {x=2} .

Example 2: Figure 4.4 contains a program which computes $B[k] = f(g(A[k]))$, $k=1,\ldots,M$ using the producer-consumer scheme of Figure 4.2. Figure 4.5a-c gives the outline of a proof for this program. Note the use of auxiliary variables sent and received. The variables in the program fall into the categories below:

$$\begin{aligned}
\text{Var(par f g)} &= \{\text{A,B,inpointer,outpointer,count,x,y,i,j,sent,received}\} \\
\text{R(par f g)} &= \{\text{inpointer,outpointer,count,buffer}\} \\
V_1\text{(par f g)} &= \{\text{A,inpointer,x,i,sent}\} \\
V_2\text{(par f g)} &= \{\text{A,B,outpointer,y,j,received}\} \\
\text{Proof-var(Bufman)} &= \{\text{A,inpointer,outpointer,count,sent,received,y}\}
\end{aligned}$$

The reader can verify that the assertions in Figure 4.5 are Einmischungsfrei, and that they lead to a proof. The only nontrivial part is showing that

$$\text{buffer}[k \bmod N]=g(A[k]),\ \text{received}<k\leq\text{sent}$$

is true after the producer's critical section; the fact that $\text{sent}-\text{received}=\text{count}<N$ is needed to show that the store operation does not erase a value which is still needed.

It is often useful to express a program proof using assertion functions like the ones defined in the last two chapters.

4.15. Definition: Suppose pre and post are functions which map components of a program S to assertions, and I maps resources to assertions. They are assertion functions for {P} S {Q} iff they obey the following restrictions for each component S' of S .

```
fg3: begin
    inpointer:=outpointer:=count:=0;
    i:=j:=1;
    par f g: resource Bufman(inpointer,outpointer,count,buffer): cobegin
        producer: while  i≤M  do
            begin  x:=g(A[i]);
                    add: with Bufman when count<N do
                        begin inpointer:=(inpointer+1) mod N;
                              buffer[inpointer]:=x;
                              count:=count+1
                        end
                    i:=i+1;
            end
    //
        consumer: while  j≤M  do
            begin remove: with Bufman when count>0 do
                        begin outpoint:=(outpointer+1) mod N;
                              y:=buffer[outpointer];
                              count:=count-1
                        end
                    B[j]:=f(y);
                    j:=j+1
            end
    coend
end
```

Figure 4.4. Computation of $B[k] = f(g(A[k]))$, $k = 1,\ldots,M$.

```
{M≥0}

fg3: begin comment sent and received are auxiliary variables;
     inpointer:=outpointer:=count:=0;
     i:=j:=1;
     sent:=received:=0;
     {I(Bufman) Λ i=sent+1=1 Λ j=received+1=1 Λ M≥0}
     par f g: resource Bufman(inpointer,outpointer,count,buffer):
         cobegin producer // consumer coend
     {I(Bufman) Λ received=M Λ B[k]=f(g(A[k])), k=1,...,M}
     end
{B[k]=f(g(A[k])), k=1,...,M}


where  I(Bufman) = {0≤count≤N Λ count=sent-received Λ inpointer=sent mod N
                    Λ outpointer=received mod N Λ buffer[k mod N] =
                    g(A[k]), received<k≤sent}
```

Figure 4.5a. An Informal Proof of fg3 (main program).

```
{i=sent+1=1 ∧ i≤M+1}
producer: while  i≤M  do
     {i=sent+1 ∧ i≤M}
     begin  x:=g(A[i]);
            {i=sent+1 ∧ i≤M ∧ x=g(A[i])}
            add: with Bufman when count<N do
               {i=sent+1 ∧ i≤M ∧ x=g(A[i]) ∧ I(Bufman) ∧ count<N}
               begin inpointer:=(inpointer+1) mod N;
                     buffer[inpointer]:=x;
                     count:=count+1;
                     sent:=sent+1;
               end
               {i=sent ∧ i≤M ∧ I(Bufman)};
            {i=sent ∧ i≤M}
            i:=i+1;
            {i=sent+1 ∧ i≤M+1}
     end
{i=sent+1 ∧ i≤M+1 ∧ ¬(i≤M)}
```

Figure 4.5b. Proof of fg3 (producer).

```
{j=received+1=1 ∧ j≤M+1}

consumer: while  j≤M  do

     {j=received+1 ∧ j≤M ∧ B[k]=f(g(A[k])), 1≤k<j}

     begin

          {j=received+1 ∧ j≤M ∧ B[k]=f(g(A[k])), 1≤k<j}

          remove: with Bufman when count>0 do

               {j=received+1 ∧ j≤M ∧ B[k]=f(g(A[k])), 1≤k<j

                                   ∧ I(Bufman) ∧ count>0}

               begin outpointer:=(outpointer+1) mod N;

                     y:=buffer[outpointer];

                     count:=count-1;

                     received:=received+1;

               end

               {j=received ∧ j≤M ∧ B[k]=f(g(A[k])), 1≤k<j ∧ y=g(A[j])

                                   ∧ I(Bufman)};

          {j=received ∧ j≤M ∧ B[k]=f(g(A[k])), 1≤k<j ∧ y=g(A[j])}

          B[j]:=f(y);

          {j=received ∧ j≤M ∧ B[k]=f(g(A[k])), 1≤k≤j}

          j:=j+1;

          {j=received+1 ∧ j≤M+1 ∧ B[k]=f(g(A[k])), 1≤k<j}

     end

{j=received+1 ∧ j≤M+1 ∧ (B[k]=f(g(A[k])), 1≤k<j) ∧ ¬(j≤M)}

{received=M ∧ B[k]=f(g(A[k])), 1≤k≤M}
```

Figure 4.5c. Proof of fg3 (consumer).

1)-6) Same as Definition 2.2 for sequential programs

7) if S' is <u>with</u> r <u>when</u> B <u>do</u> S_1 then

a) pre(S') ∧ B ∧ I(r) ⊢ pre(S_1)

b) post(S_1) ⊢ post(S') ∧ I(r)

8) if S' is <u>resource</u> $r_1,\ldots,r_m$: <u>cobegin</u> S_1 //...// S_n <u>coend</u> then

a) pre(S') ⊢ (pre(S_1) ∧ ... ∧ pre(S_n) ∧ I(r_1) ∧ ... ∧ I(r_m))

b) (post(S_1) ∧ ... ∧ post(S_n) ∧ I(r_1) ∧ ... ∧ I(r_m)) ⊢ post(S')

c) if T is a proper component of S' , the free variables in pre(T) and post(T) are elements of Proof-var(T)

d) the free variables of I(r) are elements of Proof-var(r) .

<u>4.16. Theorem:</u> If pre , post and I are assertion functions for {P} S {Q} , it is possible to prove {P} S {Q} .

<u>Proof:</u> Similar to proof of Theorem 2.3.

<u>4.17. Theorem:</u> If {P} S {Q} can be proved without using A8, there are assertion functions for {P} S {Q}.

<u>Proof:</u> Similar to proof of Theorem 2.4.

If the proof of {P} S {Q} uses A8 it is not always possible to find assertion functions for {P} S {Q} . For example, the proof of {x=0} add6 {x=2} gives assertion functions for add6 , with

pre(adda) = {y[1]=0}

post(adda) = {y[1]=1} .

But these are not assertion functions for add5 , which does not operate on y , and in fact there are no assertion functions for {x=0} add5 {x=2} . This will be reflected in the proof of Theorem 4.20.

4.4. Consistency.

Rules A0-A8 are consistent with the interpretive model, i.e., if {P} S {Q} can be proved, it is true in the model.

4.18. Theorem: Suppose S is an RPL program, and pre , post , and I are assertion functions for {P} S {Q} . Let S' be a component of S and α be a computation for S from state s_0 with $P[s_0]$=true . Then,

1) if S' is current after α , pre(S') is true after α ;
2) if α finishes S' , post(S') is true after α ;
3) if resource r is declared in a statement which is in execution for α , and r is not busy for α , then I(r) is true after α .

Proof: By induction on the length of α . The details are given in Chapter 6. The argument is much the same as for Theorem 3.15.

4.19. Theorem: (Consistency of A8) If {P} S' {Q} is true for the interpretive model and the requirements of A8 are satisfied, then {P} S {Q} is true for the interpretive model.

Proof: The same as Theorem 3.20, which expressed the consistency of A8 for GPL programs.

<u>4.20. Theorem</u>: (Consistency for RPL) If {P} S {Q} can be proved, it is true in the interpretive model.

<u>Proof</u>: Use induction on the number of uses of A8 in the proof of {P} S {Q} . If there are none, let pre and post be assertion functions for {P} S {Q} . Now suppose α executes S from state s_0 with $P[s_0]$=true . Then by Theorem 4.18, and the fact that post(S) $\vdash$ Q , Q[value(s_0,α)]=true , so {P} S {Q} is true in the model.

If the proof of {P} S {Q} uses A8, it can be rewritten so that all the steps using A8 appear at the end of the proof. Let {P} S' {Q} be the last step which does not use A8. {P} S' {Q} is true in the model. By Theorem 4.19, each application of A8 preserves this property. So {P} S {Q} is true in the model.

CHAPTER 5

ADDITIONAL PROPERTIES OF PARALLEL PROGRAMS

So far our work has been directed toward proving partial correctness as expressed by the formula {P} S {Q} . A number of other properties are relevant to parallel programs. Four of these -- mutual exclusion, blocking, deadlock, and termination -- will be discussed in this chapter. The techniques for verifying each of these properties rely on the assertion functions defined in Chapters 3 and 4, so the first step in each case is a partial-correctness proof.

Mutual exclusion is discussed in 5.1, blocking and deadlock in 5.2, and termination in 5.3. In most cases GPL and RPL programs are covered separately.

5.1. Mutual Exclusion.

Two statements in a program are mutually exclusive if they can not be executed at the same time.

5.1. Definition: Components S_1 and S_2 of S are *mutually exclusive* iff there is no computation for S which has both S_1 and S_2 in execution.

The next two sections present methods for proving mutual exclusion in GPL and RPL programs.

5.1.1. GPL.

Mutual exclusion for GPL programs was discussed informally in Section 3.5. At that time the primary interest was in using mutual exclusion in verifying that parallel processes are interference-free. Now we provide a general technique for proving that mutual exclusion is accomplished.

5.2. Theorem: Let pre and post be assertion functions for {true} S {Q}. Consider statements S_1 and S_2. Let P_1 and P_2 be assertions such that

$$\text{pre}(S_1') \Rightarrow P_1 \quad \text{for all components } S_1' \text{ of } S_1$$

$$\text{pre}(S_2') \Rightarrow P_2 \quad \text{for all components } S_2' \text{ of } S_2$$

Then if $P_1 \wedge P_2 \Rightarrow$ false, S_1 and S_2 are mutually exclusive.

Proof: Assume that there is a computation α which has both S_1 and S_2 in execution. Then some component S_1' of S_1 is current in α, and so is some component S_2' of S_2. By Theorem 3.15, $\text{pre}(S_1')[\text{value}(s_0,\alpha)]=\text{true}$, and $\text{pre}(S_2')[\text{value}(s_0,\alpha)]=\text{true}$. Then $(P_1 \wedge P_2)[\text{value}(s_0,\alpha)]=\text{true}$, but this is impossible since $P_1 \wedge P_2 \Rightarrow$ false. So no such α exists, and S_1 and S_2 are mutually exclusive.

As an example of the application of Theorem 5.2, consider the proof for mutual exclusion using semaphores presented in Figure 3.14. Here S_1 and S_2 are the critical sections in processes i and j, with $i \neq j$; $P_1 = \{I \wedge \text{inCS}[i]=1\}$ and $P_2 = \{I \wedge \text{inCS}[j]=1\}$. Since $P_1 \wedge P_2 \Rightarrow$ false, S_1 and S_2 are mutually exclusive. This proof depends on the auxiliary variable inCS , but the next theorem can be used to show that the critical sections in the original program (Figure 3.13) are also mutually exclusive.

5.3. Theorem: Suppose S_1' and S_2' are mutually exclusive components of a GPL program S' , and S is obtained by reduction of S' as in inference rule A8, without eliminating either S_1' or S_2' . Then S_1 and S_2 , the corresponding reductions of S_1' and S_2' , are mutually exclusive.

Proof: If not, let α be a computation for S which has S_1 and S_2 in execution. By Lemma 3.19 there is a corresponding computation α' for S' which has S_1' and S_2' in execution. But this is impossible, since S_1' and S_2' are mutually exclusive. So S_1 and S_2 are mutually exclusive.

In the semaphore example of Figure 3.14 the references to the auxiliary variable inCS can be removed one by one, to yield Figure 3.13. Applying Theorem 5.3 at each step shows that mutual exclusion is preserved.

5.1.2. RPL.

The RPL withwhen statement is designed to provide mutual exclusion for statements which operate on shared variables. However, there are times when the programmer must control the scheduling of resources directly and must provide his own code for mutual exclusion. In such cases mutual exclusion can be verified using techniques much like those used for GPL, but the problem is complicated by the restrictions on variables used in the assertion functions.

As an example, consider a standard synchronization problem, the five dining philosophers. Five philosophers sit around a circular table (see Figure 5.1), alternately thinking and eating spaghetti. The spaghetti is so long and tangled that a philosopher needs two forks to eat it, but unfortunately there are only five forks on the table. The only forks which a philosopher can use are the ones to his immediate right and left. Obviously two neighbors cannot eat at the same time. The problem is to write a program for each philosopher to provide this synchronization. Hoare's solution [Ho72] is given in Figure 5.2. The array af[0:4] indicates the number of forks available to each philosopher. In order to eat, a philosopher must wait until two forks are available; he then takes the forks and reduces the number available to each of his neighbors. Figure 5.3 gives pre- and post- assertions for some of the statements in the dining philosophers program. Note the use of an auxiliary array variable, eating[0:4] . The statements labelled "eat i" and "think i" do not change either eating or af .

We would like to use the assertions in Figure 5.3 to prove that mutual exclusion is accomplished, i.e., that two neighbors do not get to eat at the same time. The technique used will be essentially the same as for a GPL program: assume that the statements are not mutually exclusive and derive a contradiction. So suppose there is a computation α for which both eat i and eat $i \oplus 1$ are in execution. For this computation, $eating[i]=1 \wedge eating[i \oplus 1]=1$. If I(possforks) is also true, we have the desired contradiction, for

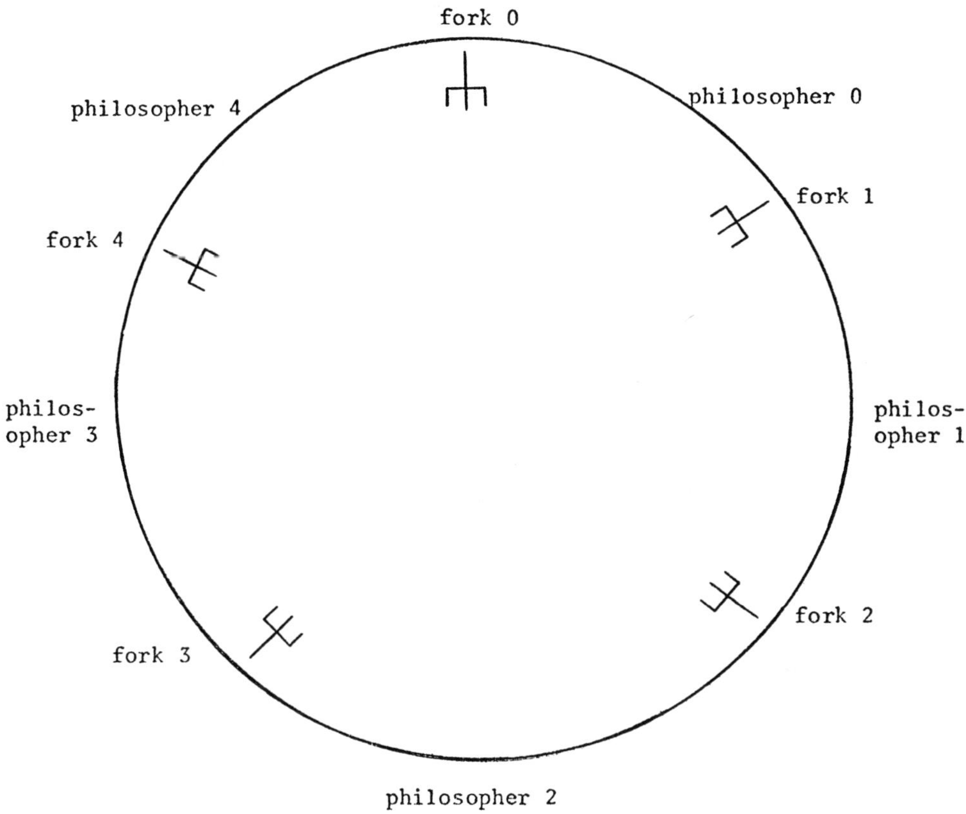

Figure 5.1. The Dining Philosophers.

```
dining philosophers: begin  comment integer array af[0:4],
        af[i] is the number of forks available to philosopher i;
    af:=2;
    resource possforks(af): cobegin
        phil 0 //...// phil 4
    coend
end

phil i: while true do
    begin
        getfork i: with possforks when af[i]=2 do
            begin af[i⊖1]=af[i⊖1] - 1;
                  af[i⊕1]=af[i⊕1] - 1;
            end;
        eat i: "eat";
        releaseforks i: with possforks do
            begin af[i⊖1]=af[i⊖1] + 1;
                  af[i⊕1]=af[i⊕1] + 1;
            end;
        think i: "think"
    end

⊕ and ⊖ indicate arithmetic modulo 5
```

Figure 5.2. Program for the Dining Philosophers.

```
{true}
dining philosophers: begin comment eating[0:4] is an auxiliary array,
         eating[i]=1 iff philosopher i is eating, 0 otherwise;
    af:=2; eating:=0;
    resource possforks(af): cobegin phil 0 //...// phil 4 coend
end
{false}


{eating[i]=0}
phil i: while true do
    begin  {eating[i]=0}
       getfork i: with possforks when af[i]=2 do
           {eating[i]=0 ∧ af[i]=2 ∧ I(possforks)}
           begin af[i⊖1]:=af[i⊖1]-1; af[i⊕1]:=af[i⊕1]-1;
                 eating[i]:=1;
           end
           {eating[i]=1 ∧ I(possforks)};
       {eating[i]=1}
       eat i: "eat";
       {eating[i]=1}
       releasefork i: with possforks do
           {eating[i]=1 ∧ I(possforks)}
           begin af[i⊖1]:=af[i⊖1]+1; af[i⊕1]:=af[i⊕1]+1;
                 eating[i]:=0;
           end
           {eating[i]=0 ∧ I(possforks)};
       {eating[i]=0}
       think i: "think"
       {eating[i]=0}
    end
    {false}
```

$$I(possforks) = \{[0 \le eating[j] \le 1 \wedge (eating[j]=1 \Rightarrow af[j]=2) \wedge af[j]=2-eating[j\ominus 1]-eating[j\oplus 1]],\ 0 \le j \le 4\}$$

Figure 5.3. Assertions for the Dining Philosophers.

$$\text{eating}[i]=1 \wedge \text{eating}[i\oplus 1]=1 \wedge I(\text{possforks})$$
$$\Rightarrow \text{af}[i]=2 \wedge \text{af}[i]<2 \Rightarrow \text{false}$$

Unfortunately I(possforks) is not necessarily true, since some other philosopher may be in the midst of executing a critical section for possforks. Nevertheless, we will show that

$$\text{eating}[i]=1 \wedge \text{eating}[i\oplus 1]=1 \wedge I(\text{possforks}) \Rightarrow \text{false}$$

guarantees that eat i and eat i⊕1 are mutually exclusive. This will be done by deriving from α another computation β for which

$$(\text{eating}[i]=1 \wedge \text{eating}[i\oplus 1]=1 \wedge I(\text{possforks}))[\text{value}(s_0,\beta)]=\text{true} .$$

Since this is a contradiction, the original computation α did not exist, and eat i and eat i⊕1 are mutually exclusive.

"Backing up" a Computation.

The technique used in obtaining β from α is the deletion of some elements of α in a way which is equivalent to "backing up" some of the processes. This technique, which was suggested by Lipton's reduction method [Li74b], will be used again in Chapter 6. It is justified by the following lemmas.

5.4. Lemma: If $\alpha = \alpha_1 S_1 S_2 \alpha_2$ is a computation for S , where S_1 is not the last statement in a critical section, and S_1 and S_2 are from different processes, then

1) $\beta = \alpha_1 S_2 S_1 \alpha_2$ is a computation for S , and
2) $\text{value}(s_0,\alpha) = \text{value}(s_0,\beta)$.

Proof: First show that S_1 does not change any variables used in S_2. To see this, suppose S_1 changes the value of x. If x is not a resource element, the syntactical restrictions prevent x from appearing in S_2. If x is an element of resource r, S_1 must be a component of a critical section for r. Since $\alpha_1 S_1$ does not finish this critical section, r is busy in $\alpha_1 S_1$. By Lemma 4.11, S_2 does not refer to x.

By similar arguments, S_2 does not change any variables used in S_1, and S_1 and S_2 are not both withwhen statements for the same resource.

Now 1-2 can be proved using induction on the length of α_2. If α_2 is empty, $\alpha = \alpha_1 S_1 S_2$ and $\beta = \alpha_1 S_2 S_1$. Since S_1 and S_2 do not modify each other's variables, they can be executed in either order with the same result, and 1 and 2 are true.

If $\alpha_2 = \alpha' S'$, let $s = \text{value}(s_0, \alpha_1 S_1 S_2 \alpha')$. By induction, $\text{value}(s_0, \alpha_1 S_2 S_1 \alpha') = s$. Then, S' is ready to execute in s, and β is a computation. Also, $\text{value}(s_0, \beta) = \text{next}(s, S') = \text{value}(s_0, \alpha)$, and 1 and 2 are satisfied.

5.5. Lemma: If $\alpha = \alpha_1 S_1 \alpha_2$ is a computation for S, where S_1 is not the last statement in a critical section, and the statements in α_2 are not from the same process as S_1, then

1) $\beta = \alpha_1 \alpha_2$ is a computation for S, and
2) if T is current after α, and T is not from the same process as S_1, T is current after β.

Proof: Lemma 5.4 can be applied several times to obtain the computation $\beta' = \alpha_1\alpha_2S_1$ with value(s_0,α) = value(s_0,β') . Letting $\beta = \alpha_1\alpha_2$ satisfies 1 and 2.

This is equivalent to "backing up" one statement in the process containing S_1 .

5.6. Lemma: If a statement S , which does not properly contain a withwhen statement, is in execution for α , there is a computation β such that

1) S is current after β ;
2) if T is current after α and T is not in the same process as S , T is current after β ;

Proof: Lemma 5.4 can be applied several times to "back up" until S is current. (Since S does not properly contain a withwhen, none of the statements to be deleted finishes a critical section.) At each step the deleted statement is a component of S , so 2 is preserved.

Proving Mutual Exclusion.

With this background we can state and prove a general theorem which can be applied to prove mutual exclusion for the dining philosophers.

5.7. Definition: r is a simple resource in S iff no withwhen statement for r in S properly contains another withwhen statement.

5.8. Theorem: Suppose S is an RPL program with assertion functions pre, post, and I for {true} S {Q}, S_1 and S_2 are components of S , and P_1 and P_2 are assertions such that

$pre(S_1') \Rightarrow P_1$ for all components S_1' of S_1 .

$pre(S_2') \Rightarrow P_2$ for all components S_2' of S_2 .

Let $R = \{r$: r is a simple resource declared in a statement containing S_1 and S_2 , and neither S_1 nor S_2 is a proper component of a <u>withwhen</u> statement for $r\}$.

Then if $P_1 \wedge P_2 \wedge (\bigwedge_{r \in R} I(r)) \Rightarrow$ false, S_1 and S_2 are mutually exclusive.

<u>Proof</u>: Suppose S_1 and S_2 are not mutually exclusive. Then there is a computation α such that S_1 and S_2 are in execution for α . We will derive a computation β which has S_1 and S_2 in execution, and if $r \in R$, r is not busy in β . Then by Theorem 4.18, $(\bigwedge_{r \in R} I(r))[value(s_0,\beta)]=true$.

By Lemma 4.11, if r is busy in α some <u>withwhen</u> statement for r , say S_0 , is in execution for α . Since r is a simple resource, Lemma 5.6 can be applied to back up until S_0 is ready to execute. If α' is the new computation, r is not busy in α' . Since S_1 and S_2 are not components of S_0 , they are still in execution for α' . Also, if r' is a resource which is not busy in α , it is not busy in α' , since no statements which end critical sections were deleted. So this operation can be repeated for each $r \in R$ to derive the desired computation β .

Since S_1 is in execution for β , some component S_1' of S_1 is current for β . Then by Theorem 4.18, $pre(S_1)[value(s_0,\beta)]=true$.

Similarly, $pre(S_2)[value(s_0,\beta)]=true$. But then $(P_1 \wedge P_2 \wedge (\bigwedge_{r\epsilon R} I(r)))[value(s_0,\beta)]=true$. Since this is impossible, S_1 and S_2 are mutually exclusive.

Example: Returning to the dining philosophers problem, let

$$P_1 = \{eating[i]=1\}$$

$$P_2 = \{eating[i\oplus 1]=1\}$$

$$R = \{possforks\}$$

Then $P_1 \wedge P_2 \wedge (\bigwedge_{r\epsilon R} I(r)) \Rightarrow false$, and "eat i" and "eat i⊕1" are mutually exclusive in the program with auxiliary variables. To show that they are mutually exclusive in the original program we need the following theorem.

5.9. Theorem: Suppose S_1' and S_2' are mutually exclusive components of an RPL program S' , and S is obtained by reduction of S' as in inference rule A8, without eliminating either S_1' or S_2' . Then S_1 and S_2 , the corresponding reductions of S_1' and S_2' , are mutually exclusive.

Proof: Same as Theorem 5.3.

User-Defined Critical Sections.

Another standard synchronization problem, called the readers and writers problem, involves a number of processes sharing a file. Any number of readers may have access to the file at the same time, but a writer must have exclusive access. Figure 5.4 gives a solution to the readers and writers problem due to Brinch Hansen [Br72a]; it gives a higher priority to the writers. Figure 5.5a-c shows some pre and post assertions for the program using auxiliary variables reading, waiting, and writing. Applying Theorem 5.8 we can see that reader i excludes writer j, since

$$\text{reading}[i]=1 \wedge \text{writing}[j]=1 \wedge I(\text{control})$$
$$\Rightarrow ar>0 \wedge aw>0 \wedge (ar=0 \vee aw=0) \Rightarrow \text{false} .$$

Also, writers exclude each other, since

$$\text{writing}[i]=1 \wedge \text{writing}[j]=1 \wedge I(\text{control})$$
$$\Rightarrow aw\geq 2 \wedge aw\leq 1 \Rightarrow \text{false}$$

if $i \neq j$. So, the code provided does synchronize access to the file as required.

Suppose now that the null statements labelled "read i" and "write j" are replaced by statements which actually operate on the file. In order to obey the syntax requirements of RPL, they must use <u>withwhen</u> statements, even though this prevents reader processes from using the file simultaneously. Actually the <u>withwhen</u> statements are redundant; the statements which use "control" are like a programmer-defined <u>withwhen</u> statement for the file. This suggests an extension of RPL to include programmer-defined critical sections. The programmer could specify the code to be executed when acquiring and releasing a

```
RW: begin  ww:=ar:=0;
      resource control(ww,ar): cobegin
            reader_1 //...// reader_n //
            writer_1 //...// writer_m
      coend
end

reader i: while true do
      begin
            startread i: with control when ww=0 do ar:=ar+1;
            read i: ;
            finishread i: with control do ar:=ar-1;
      end

writer j: while true do
      begin
            ask write j: with control do ww:=ww+1;
            start write j: with control when ar=0 Λ aw=0 do aw:=aw+1;
            write j: ;
            finish write j: with control do begin aw:=aw-1; ww:=ww-1 end
      end
```

ww = number of waiting or active writers
ar = number of active readers
aw = number of active writers

Figure 5.4. Readers and Writers.

```
{true}
begin ww:=ar:=0;
    comment  reading[i]=1  if reader i is active, 0  otherwise
             writing[i]=1  if writer i is active, 0  otherwise
             waiting[i]=1  if writer i is waiting or active,
                                    0  otherwise;
    reading:=writing:=waiting:=0;
    {I(control) ∧ ∀i(reading[i]=0) ∧ ∀j(waiting[j]=writing[j]=0)}
    resource control(ar,ww): cobegin
        reader 1 //...// reader n //
        writer 1 //...// writer m
    coend
end
{false}
```

$$I(\text{control}) = \{ar = \sum_i \text{reading}[i] \wedge ww = \sum_j \text{waiting}[j] \wedge aw = \sum_j \text{writing}[j]$$

$$\wedge\ 0 \le aw \le 1 \wedge (ar=0 \vee aw=0) \wedge (\text{writing}[i]=1 \Rightarrow \text{waiting}[i]=1)$$

$$\wedge\ 0 \le \text{waiting}[j],\ \text{writing}[j],\ \text{reading}[i] \le 1\}$$

Figure 5.5a. Assertions for Readers and Writers (main program).

```
{reading[i]=0}
reader i: while true do
     begin
          {reading[i]=0}
          start read i: with control when ww=0 do
               begin ar:=ar+1; reading[i]:=1  end;
          {reading[i]=1}
          read i: ;
          {reading[i]=1}
          finish read i: with control do
               begin ar:=ar-1; reading[i]:=0  end;
          {reading[i]=0}
     end
{false}
```

$$I(\text{control}) = \{ar = \sum_i \text{reading}[i] \wedge ww = \sum_j \text{waiting}[j] \wedge aw = \sum_j \text{writing}[j] \wedge$$
$$0 \leq aw \leq 1 \wedge (ar=0 \vee aw=0) \wedge (\text{writing}[j]=1 \Rightarrow \text{waiting}[j]=1) \wedge$$
$$0 \leq \text{waiting}[j], \text{writing}[j], \text{reading}[i] \leq 1\}$$

Figure 5.5b. Assertions for Readers and Writers (reader i).

```
{waiting[j]=writing[j]=0}
writer j: while true do
      begin
          {waiting[j]=writing[j]=0}
          ask write j: with control do
              begin ww:=ww+1; waiting[j]:=1  end;
          {waiting[j]=1 ∧ writing[j]=0}
          start write j: with control when ar=0 ∧ aw=0 do
              begin aw:=aw+1; writing[j]:=1 end;
          {waiting[j]=writing[j]=1}
          write j: ;
          {waiting[j]=writing[j]=1}
          finish write j: with control do
              begin ww:=ww-1; aw:=aw-1; waiting[j]:=writing[j]:=0 end
          {waiting[j]=writing[j]=0}
      end
{false}
```

$$I(\text{control}) = \{ar = \sum_i \text{reading}[i] \wedge ww = \sum_j \text{waiting}[j] \wedge aw = \sum_j \text{writing}[j]$$
$$\wedge\ 0 \le aw \le 1 \wedge (ar=0 \vee aw=0) \wedge (\text{writing}[j]=1 \Rightarrow \text{waiting}[j]=1)$$
$$\wedge\ 0 \le \text{waiting}[j],\ \text{writing}[j],\ \text{reading}[i] \le 1\}$$

Figure 5.5c. Assertions for Readers and Writers (writer j).

resource. As long as this code guaranteed mutual exclusion, the programmer-defined critical sections could be used in programs and proofs in the same way as the standard withwhen.

There are a number of ways in which such an extension could be incorporated in RPL. One possibility is the declaration of a monitor somewhat like Hoare's [Ho74a] for each resource. The programmer could either provide his own code for the monitor or accept a standard system implementation. We are currently working on syntactic constructs to provide for this feature.

5.2. Blocking.

Another problem which is peculiar to parallel processes is that a program can be forced to stop before it has accomplished its purpose. This can happen in GPL or RPL programs because of the await and withwhen statements.

5.10. Definition: If S' is a component of a GPL or RPL program S , and α is a computation for S , S' is blocked for α iff S' is in execution for α but no component of S' is ready to execute after α .

In other words, at least one component of S' is current for α , but none of the current components of S' are ready to execute. For a GPL program this means that all the current components of S' are await statements; for an RPL program they must be withwhen statements.

5.11. Definition: If S' is a component of the GPL or RPL program S , S' can not be blocked with starting condition P iff there is no computation which starts with P true and has S' blocked. S' can not be blocked if it can not be blocked with starting condition {true} .

In many cases blocking is harmless: an await or withwhen statement may be blocked and then unblocked many times during program execution. However, if an entire program is blocked, or if a set of parallel processes is deadlocked in acquiring resources, the program cannot recover. In Sections 5.2.1 and 5.2.3 we describe techniques for proving that programs cannot become blocked, while in 5.2.2 a well-known method for avoiding deadlock is related to RPL programs.

5.2.1. Program Blocking in GPL.

A GPL program can become blocked if every parallel process is stopped at an await statement whose condition is false. In order to prove that blocking is impossible in a particular program we assume that it occurs and derive a contradiction. We first consider the relatively easy case of a program with only one parallel statement.

Single Parallel Statement:

5.12. Theorem: Suppose GPL program S contains one parallel statement T = cobegin $T_1//\ldots//T_n$ coend , and let pre and post be assertion functions for {P} S {Q} . Let T_j^i = await B_j^i then ... be the await statements in T_i . Then if

$$D_1 = \bigwedge_{i=1}^{n} (\text{post}(T_i) \vee (\bigvee_j (\text{pre}(T_j^i) \wedge \neg B_j^i)))$$

$$D_2 = \bigvee_i \bigvee_j (\text{pre}(T_j^i) \wedge \neg B_j^i)$$

and $D_1 \wedge D_2 \Rightarrow \text{false}$, S cannot be blocked with starting condition P .

<u>Proof</u>: Suppose S is blocked for the computation α which starts with P true. Since S can only be blocked at <u>await</u> statements in T , α has begun parallel execution of the T_i . For each process T_i , either α has finished T_i and $\text{post}(T_i)[\text{value}(s_0,\alpha)]=\text{true}$ (Theorem 3.15), or T_i is blocked at one of T_j^i and $(\text{pre}(T_j^i) \wedge \neg B_j^i)[\text{value}(s_0,\alpha)]=\text{true}$. So $D_1[\text{value}(s_0,\alpha)]=\text{true}$. Since at least one T_i is blocked for α , $D_2[\text{value}(s_0,\alpha)]=\text{true}$. But this is a contradiction, since $D_1 \wedge D_2 \Rightarrow \text{false}$, so no such α exists.

Note that if S contains no <u>await</u> statements, D_2 is the empty union, which conventionally has the value false; in this case S cannot become blocked.

<u>Examples</u>: Chapter 3 contained several examples of programs in GPL. Findpos (Figure 3.3) cannot be blocked since it contains no <u>await</u> statements. In addl (Figure 3.8) both of the <u>await</u> statements have $B_j^i \equiv \text{true}$. The expression D_2 becomes

$$D_2 = (\text{pre(adda)} \wedge \neg\text{true}) \vee (\text{pre(addb)} \wedge \neg\text{true})$$

$$= \text{false} .$$

Then $D_1 \wedge D_2 \Rightarrow \text{false}$, and addl cannot become blocked.

In the mutual exclusion program (Figure 3.14) each S_i has two <u>await</u> statements:

$$T_1^i = \underline{\text{await}} \;\; \text{mutex}>0 \;\; \underline{\text{then}} \; \ldots$$

$$T_2^i = \underline{\text{await}} \; \text{true} \; \underline{\text{then}} \; \ldots$$

Then,

$$D_1 = \bigwedge_{i=1}^{N} (\text{post}(S_i) \vee (\text{pre}(T_1^i) \wedge \text{mutex}\leq 0) \vee (\text{pre}(T_2^i) \wedge \text{false})) \quad .$$

$$= \bigwedge_{i=1}^{N} (\text{false} \vee (\text{pre}(T_1^i) \wedge \text{mutex}\leq 0) \vee \text{false})$$

$$= \bigwedge_{i=1}^{N} (I \wedge \text{inCS}[i]=0 \wedge \text{mutex}\leq 0)$$

$$\Rightarrow \text{mutex}\leq 0 \wedge \text{mutex}=1 - \sum_{i=1}^{N} \text{inCS}[i] \wedge \forall i(\text{inCS}[i]=0)$$

$$\Rightarrow \text{mutex}\leq 0 \wedge \text{mutex}=1$$

$$\Rightarrow \text{false} \; .$$

Thus, this method of using semaphores to implement mutual exclusion is safe from blocking.

We next consider blocking in programs with nested parallel statements. This is essentially the same as the case with no nesting, but the details are more cumbersome.

<u>5.13. Theorem</u>: Suppose S is a GPL program with assertion functions pre and post for {P} S {Q} . For each parallel statement T =

cobegin $T_1//\ldots//T_n$ coend in S , let T_j^i = await B_j^i then ... be the await statements in T_i which are not components of another parallel statement inside T_i . Let

$$D_1(T) = \bigwedge_i (\mathrm{post}(T_i) \vee (\bigvee_j (\mathrm{pre}(T_j^i) \wedge \neg B_j^i)))$$

$$D_2(T) = \bigvee_i \bigvee_j (\mathrm{pre}(T_j^i) \wedge \neg B_j^i) \ .$$

Then, if $D_1(T) \wedge D_2(T) \Rightarrow$ false for all parallel T in S , S cannot be blocked with initial condition P .

Proof: Suppose S is blocked for some computation α which starts with P true. Then at least one parallel statement is blocked for α . Let T be a parallel statement which is blocked for α with no parallel statement inside T blocked for α . Then T must be blocked at one or more of the T_j^i , and $D_1(T) \wedge D_2(T)[\mathrm{value}(s_0,\alpha)]$=true as in Theorem 5.12. Since this is a contradiction, S cannot be blocked.

Example: Figure 5.6 is a program which uses 2 semaphores for mutual exclusion. In an earlier example we showed that single parallel statements which use semaphores in this way cannot be blocked. Similar reasoning can be applied to each of the parallel statements in the program nested1; since neither of them can be blocked, the program cannot be blocked.

Unfortunately Theorem 5.13 is not strong enough in many cases. Figure 5.7 shows a program "nested2" which cannot be blocked. However,

```
nested1: begin  m1:=m2:=1;
     outer: cobegin
         S1: begin  P(m1);
                    critical section 1;
                    V(m1)
             end
     //
         S2: begin  P(m1);
                    critical section 2;
                    inner: cobegin
                        S21: begin P(m2); critical section 3; V(m2)  end
                    //
                        S22: begin P(m2); critical section 4; V(m2)  end
                    coend;
                    V(m1)
             end
     coend
end
```

Figure 5.6. Nested Parallel Statements 1.

```
nested2: begin ml:=1;
     outer: cobegin
          S1: begin  wait1: P(ml);
                     critical section 1;
                     V(ml)
              end
     //
          inner: cobegin
               S2: begin  wait2: P(ml);
                          critical section 2;
                          V(ml)
                   end
          //
               S3: begin  wait3: P(ml);
                          critical section 3;
                          V(ml)
                   end
          coend
     coend
end
```

Figure 5.7. Nested Parallel Statements 2.

the parallel statement "inner" can be blocked when S1 is executing its critical section, so Theorem 5.13 does not apply. The following more general theorem can be used in such cases.

5.14. Theorem: Suppose S is a GPL program with assertion functions pre and post for {P} S {Q} . For each parallel statement T = cobegin $T_1 // \ldots // T_n$ coend let T_j^i = await B_j^i then ... be as in Theorem 5.13, and let S_k^i be the parallel statements in T_i which are not components of another parallel statement inside T_i . Let

$$D(T_i) = (\bigvee_j (pre(T_j^i) \wedge \neg B_j^i) \vee (\bigvee_k D_1(S_k^i))$$

$$D_1(T) = \bigwedge_i (post(T_i) \vee D(T_i))$$

$$D_2(T) = \bigvee_i D(T_i) .$$

Then, if $D_1(T) \wedge D_2(T) \Rightarrow$ false , for every parallel T which is not contained in another parallel statement, S cannot be blocked with initial condition P .

Proof: Suppose S is blocked for some computation α which starts with P true. First we will show that if T is a parallel component of S which is blocked for α , $D_1(T) \wedge D_2(T)[value(s_0,\alpha)]$=true . First, suppose that T contains no nested parallel statements. In this case, $D_1(T)$ and $D_2(T)$ reduce to D_1 and D_2 of Theorem 5.13, and $D_1 \wedge D_2[value(s_0,\alpha)]$=true . If T contains nested parallel statements, consider the state of each T_i after α . There are three possibilities:

1) α finishes T_i , and $post(T_i)[value(s_0,\alpha)]=true$.

2) T_i is blocked at one of the T^i_j , and $(pre(T^i_j) \wedge \neg B^i_j)[value(s_0,\alpha)]=$ true .

3) T_i is stopped inside some S^i_k , and by induction $(D_1(S^i_k) \wedge D_2(S^i_k))[value(s_0,\alpha)]=true$.

This gives $D_1(T)[value(s_0,\alpha)]=true$, and since at least one T_i must be blocked for α , $D_2(T)[value(s_0,\alpha)]=true$. Then if T is blocked for α , $D_1(T) \wedge D_2(T)[value(s_0,\alpha)]=true$.

Now if S is blocked for α , at least one of the outermost parallel statements T' is blocked for α , and $D_1(T') \wedge D_2(T')\cdot[value(s_0,\alpha)]=true$. But this is a contradiction, so no such α exists.

Note that Theorem 5.13 describes the special case of Theorem 5.14 in which $D_1(T) \wedge D_2(T) \Rightarrow false$ for all parallel T .

This theorem can be used to prove that the program nested2 in Figure 5.7 cannot be blocked. Figure 5.8 shows some pre and post assertions which can be derived by expressing P and V with <u>await</u> statements as done in Figure 3.14. Then

$$D_1(inner) = [post(S2) \vee (pre(wait2) \wedge mutex \leq 0)]$$
$$\wedge\ [post(S3) \vee (pre(wait3) \wedge mutex \leq 0)]$$
$$\Rightarrow (inCS[2]=inCS[3]=0) \wedge I$$

$$D_1(outer) = [post(S1) \vee (pre(wait1) \wedge mutex \leq 0)]$$
$$\wedge\ [post(inner) \vee D_1(inner)]$$
$$\Rightarrow (inCS[1]=inCS[2]=inCS[3]=0 \wedge I)$$
$$\Rightarrow mutex=1$$

```
{I ∧ inCS[i]=0}
Si: begin
    {I ∧ inCS[i]=0}
    wait i: P(m1);
    {I ∧ inCS[i]=1}
    critical section i;
    {I ∧ inCS[i]=1}
    V(m1);
    {I ∧ inCS[i]=0}
    end
{I ∧ inCS[i]=0}
```

$$I = \{m1 = 1 - \sum_i inCS[i] \wedge m1 \geq 0 \wedge (0 \leq inCS[i] \leq 1),\ i=1,2,3\}$$

Figure 5.8. Some Assertions for S_i of Figure 5.7.

$$D_2(\text{outer}) = [\text{pre(wait1)} \wedge \text{mutex} \leq 0] \vee [\text{pre(wait2)} \wedge \text{mutex} \leq 0]$$

$$\vee\ [\text{pre(wait3)} \wedge \text{mutex} \leq 0]$$

$$\Rightarrow \text{mutex} \leq 0$$

$$D_1(\text{outer}) \wedge D_2(\text{outer}) \Rightarrow \text{false} .$$

So the program cannot be blocked.

This completes the discussion of blocking in GPL programs. In the next two sections we consider two kinds of blocking for RPL programs.

5.2.2. Deadlock in RPL.

Deadlock is a particular kind of blocking which can occur when parallel processes are competing for resources. It occurs when a set of processes reach a state in which each is trying to acquire a resource which is already controlled by another. In an RPL program resources are acquired by withwhen statements, and deadlock can be related to withwhen.

5.15. Definition: An RPL program S is deadlocked for a computation α iff there are components S_i , $1 \leq i \leq n$ of S such that each S_i is blocked at a withwhen statement for a resource r_i , and some S_j is blocked inside a withwhen statement for r_i , i.e., S_j has already acquired r_i .

As a simple example consider the program

```
resource  r1,r2: cobegin
        S1: with  r1  do with  r2  do . . .
      // S2: with  r2  do with  r1  do . . .
coend
```

If S1 acquires r1 and S2 acquires r2 neither statement can proceed and the program is deadlocked.

5.16. Definition: An RPL program S is *deadlock-free* iff there is no computation for which S is deadlocked.

There is a well-known technique for avoiding deadlock; each process must request and release resources in some standard order. In an RPL program this can be accomplished by restrictions on the nesting of *withwhen* statements.

5.17. Theorem: An RPL program S is deadlock-free if its resources can be put in an order $r_{i_1},\ldots,r_{i_m}$ such that no *withwhen* statement using r_{i_j} properly contains a *withwhen* statement using r_{i_k} with $k \leq j$.

Proof: Suppose S is deadlocked for the computation α . Let S_i , $1 \leq i \leq n$ be the components of S which are deadlocked, and let j be the largest index of a resource such that one of the S_i is blocked at a *withwhen* statement for r_{i_j} . Then some S_i is blocked inside a critical section for r_{i_j} say at a *withwhen* statement for r_{i_k} . Then $k \geq j$, but this contradicts the choice of j . So S cannot be deadlocked.

Of course, there are other ways of avoiding deadlock, but the technique above is especially convenient since it can be checked syntactically. Note that a program with no nested critical sections is deadlock-free.

Example: Figure 5.9a and b gives two additional solutions to the dining philosophers problem; they are also due to Hoare [Ho72]. The first is in danger of deadlock, since if the five philosophers simultaneously pick up the fork on the right no one will be able to pick up his second fork. The next solution avoids this problem by following the discipline of Theorem 5.17, so it is deadlock-free (the order is fork0, fork1, ... , fork4). However, it has the undesirable feature that when philosopher 4 is eating, the other four may be forced to wait until he has finished. The solution in Figure 5.2 is preferable, because it does not stop a philosopher from eating unless one of his neighbors is eating.

5.2.3. Program Blocking in RPL.

Deadlock is one way in which a program can be blocked; blocking can also occur if all processes are waiting at withwhen statements for conditions which are not satisfied. This situation is related to blocking in GPL programs as presented in 5.2.1, but it is complicated by the fact that the statement with r when B do S can be blocked either because r is busy or because B is false. When a deadlock-free program is blocked we can assume that at least one statement is blocked because B is false.

```
resource fork 0, fork 1, fork 2, fork 3, fork 4:
     cobegin  phil 0 //...// phil 4  coend

     phil i: while true do
                 with fork i do  with fork i⊕1 do  "eat"
```

Figure 5.9a. Dining Philosophers -- Solution 2.

```
if  0≤i≤3
     phil i: while true do
                 with fork i do  with fork i⊕1 do  "eat"

     phil 4: while true do
                 with fork 0 do  with fork 4 do  "eat"
```

Figure 5.9b. Dining Philosophers -- Solution 3.

5.18. Lemma: If S is a deadlock-free RPL program which is blocked for α , there is at least one statement S' = with r when B do ... which is blocked for α with $(\text{pre}(S') \wedge \neg B \wedge I(r))[\text{value}(s_0,\alpha)]=\text{true}$.

Proof: Let T_i = with r_i when B_i do ... be a list of the withwhen statements at which S is blocked. If all the r_i are busy for α , S is deadlocked, so there is at least one r_i which is not busy for α . This implies that $I(r_i)[\text{value}(s_0,\alpha)]=\text{true}$. Also, since S is blocked at T_i , $(\text{pre}(T_i) \wedge \neg B_i)[\text{value}(s_0,\alpha)]=\text{true}$.

Now we derive some results which can be used to prove that RPL programs do not become blocked. The first case considered is programs with only one parallel statement.

Single Parallel Statement.

5.19. Theorem: Suppose S is a deadlock-free RPL program containing one parallel statement T = resource $r_1,\ldots,r_m$: cobegin $T_1//\ldots//T_n$ coend , and pre, post, and I are assertion functions for {P} S {Q} . Let the withwhen statements in T_i be T^i_j = with r^i_j when B^i_j do ... Define

$$R = \{r:\ r \text{ a simple resource of } S \text{ (Definition 5.7)}\}$$

$$P^i_j = \neg B^i_j \text{ , if } r^i_j \in R$$

$$= \text{true, otherwise}$$

$$D(T_i) = \bigvee_j (\text{pre}(T^i_j) \wedge P^i_j)$$

$$D_1 = \bigwedge_i (\text{post}(T_i) \vee D(T_i))$$

$$D_2 = \bigvee_i \bigvee_j (\text{pre}(T_j^i) \wedge \neg B_j^i \wedge I(r_j^i))$$

$$D_3 = \bigwedge_{r \in R} I(r)$$

Then, if $D_1 \wedge D_2 \wedge D_3 \Rightarrow \text{false}$, S cannot be blocked with initial condition P .

Proof: The argument is essentially the same as for Theorem 5.12. Suppose S is blocked for α which starts with P true. First, note that if r is a simple resource, control cannot be blocked inside a critical section for r , so r is not busy for α . Thus, $D_3[\text{value}(s_0,\alpha)]=\text{true}$.

Each of the T_i is either finished or blocked after α . If T_i is blocked, it is trying to enter some T_j^i , so $\text{pre}(T_j^i)[\text{value}(s_0,\alpha)]= \text{true}$. If r is a simple resource, it is not busy for α , so T is blocked because $B_j^i[\text{value}(s_0,\alpha)]=\text{false}$. Thus, if T_i is blocked, $D(T_i)$ is true. Since each T_i is either finished or blocked, D_1 is true, and by Lemma 5.18, D_2 is true. So, $D_1 \wedge D_2 \wedge D_3[\text{value}(s_0,\alpha)]= \text{true}$. But this is impossible, so S cannot be blocked.

There are several examples in Chapters 4 and 5 of programs which cannot be blocked.

Dining Philosophers (Figure 5.3): The program has no nested withwhen statements and so is deadlock-free.

$$R = \{possforks\}$$

$$D(phil\ i) = (pre(getfork\ i) \wedge af[i] \neq 2)$$

$$\vee\ (pre(releasefork\ i) \wedge false)$$

$$= eating[i]=0 \wedge af[i] \neq 2$$

$$D_1 = \bigwedge_i (post(T_i) \vee D(phil\ i))$$

$$= \bigwedge_i (false \vee (eating[i]=0 \wedge af[i] \neq 2))$$

$$= \bigwedge_i (eating[i]=0 \wedge af[i] \neq 2)$$

$$D_3 = I(possforks)$$

$$\Rightarrow (0 \leq eating[i] \leq 1 \wedge af[i]=2-eating[i \ominus 1]-eating[i \oplus 1])$$

$$D_1 \wedge D_3 \Rightarrow \bigwedge_i (af[i] \neq 2 \wedge af[i]=2) \Rightarrow false\ .$$

so the dining philosophers program cannot be blocked.

Readers and Writers (Figure 5.4): A very similar proof shows that this program cannot be blocked.

Producer and Consumer (Figure 4.5): Again, there are no nested withwhen statements, and the program is deadlock-free.

$$R = \{\text{Bufman}\}$$

$$D(\text{producer}) = \text{pre(add)} \wedge \text{count} \geq N$$

$$\Rightarrow \text{sent} < M \wedge \text{count} \geq N$$

$$D(\text{consumer}) = \text{pre(remove)} \wedge \text{count} \leq 0$$

$$\Rightarrow \text{received} < M \wedge \text{count} \leq 0$$

$$D_1 = (\text{post(consumer)} \vee D(\text{consumer})) \wedge (\text{post(producer)} \vee D(\text{producer}))$$

$$\Rightarrow (\text{sent}=M \vee (\text{sent}<M \wedge \text{count} \geq N)) \wedge (\text{received}=M \vee (\text{received}<M \wedge \text{count} \leq 0))$$

$$D_2 = D(\text{consumer}) \vee D(\text{producer})$$

$$\Rightarrow \text{sent}<M \vee \text{received}<M$$

$$D_3 = I(\text{Bufman}) \Rightarrow \text{count}=\text{sent}-\text{received}$$

Consider the value of $D_1 \wedge D_2 \wedge D_3$ for the two cases of D_2 .

Case 1: sent<M

$$D_1 \wedge \text{sent}<M \wedge D_3 \Rightarrow (\text{sent}<M \wedge \text{count} \geq N) \wedge (\text{received}=M \vee (\text{received}<M \wedge \text{count} \leq 0)) \wedge \text{count}= \text{sent}-\text{received}$$

$$\Rightarrow \text{sent}<M \wedge \text{count} \geq N \wedge \text{received}=M \wedge \text{count}=\text{sent}-\text{received}, \quad \text{if } N>0$$

$$\Rightarrow \text{count} \geq N \wedge \text{count}<0 \Rightarrow \text{false, if } N \geq 0 .$$

Case 2: received<M

$D_1 \wedge \text{received}<M \wedge D_3$

$\Rightarrow (\text{sent}=M \vee (\text{sent}<M \wedge \text{count}\geq N)) \wedge (\text{received}<M \wedge \text{count}\leq 0)$

$\wedge\ \text{count}=\text{sent}-\text{received}$

$\Rightarrow \text{sent}=M \wedge \text{received}<M \wedge \text{count}\leq 0 \wedge \text{count}=\text{sent}-\text{received}$, if $N>0$

$\Rightarrow \text{count}\leq 0 \wedge \text{count}>0$

$\Rightarrow$ false .

So $D_1 \wedge D_2 \wedge D_3 \Rightarrow$ false if $N>0$. This leads to the reasonable requirement that the buffer used for communication must have at least one element so that the program cannot be blocked.

<u>Nested Parallel Statements.</u>

Theorem 5.19 applies only to programs in which there are no nested parallel statements. The theorem below is more general, and is analagous to Theorem 5.14.

<u>5.20. Theorem</u>: Let S be a deadlock-free RPL program with assertion functions pre, post, and I for {P} S {Q} . For each parallel component T = <u>resource</u> $r_1,\ldots,r_m$: <u>cobegin</u> $T_1//\ldots//T_n$ <u>coend</u> , let S_k^i be the parallel statements in T_i which are not proper components of another parallel statement inside T_i , and let T_j^i be the <u>withwhen</u> statements of T_i which are not contained in any S_k^i . Define

$R(T)$ = {r: r a simple resource declared in a statement which contains T}

$P_j^i = \neg B_j^i$, if $r_j^i \in R(T)$

= true, otherwise

$$D(T_i) = (\bigvee_j (pre(T_j^i) \wedge P_j^i)) \vee (\bigvee_k D_1(S_k^i))$$

$$D_1(T) = \bigwedge_i (post(T_i) \vee D(T_i))$$

$$D_2(T) = \bigvee_{\substack{T'=\underline{with}\ r\ \underline{when}\ B\ \underline{do}\ \ldots \\ \text{a component of } T}} (pre(T' \wedge \neg B \wedge I(r))$$

$$D_3(T) = \bigwedge_{r \in R(T)} I(r)$$

Then if $D_1(T) \wedge D_2(T) \wedge D_3(T) \Rightarrow$ false for each parallel T which is not a proper component of another parallel statement, S cannot be blocked with initial condition P .

Proof: Suppose S is blocked for some computation α which starts with P true. First, we will show that if T is a parallel component of S which is blocked for α , $D_1(T) \wedge D_2(T) \wedge D_3(T)[value(s_0,\alpha)]=$ true .

First, note that no process can be blocked inside a critical section for a simple resource, so no simple resource is busy for α , which implies $D_3(T)[value(s_0,\alpha)]=true$.

Next, by Lemma 5.18, $D_2[value(s_0,\alpha)]=true$.

Finally, $D_1(T)$ holds after α . If T does not contain any nested parallel statement, $D_1(T)$ reduces to D_1 of Theorem 5.19, and by similar reasoning $D_1[value(s_0,\alpha)]=true$. If T does contain parallel statements, there are three possible states for each T_i

1) α finishes T_i , and $post(T_i)[value(s_0,\alpha)]=true$.

2) T_i is blocked at some T_j^i , and $(pre(T_j^i) \wedge P_j^i)[value(s_0,\alpha)]=true$.

3) T_i is blocked inside some S_k^i , and by induction $D_1(S_k^i)[value(s_0,\alpha)]=true$.

Combining 1)-3) yields $D_1(T)[value(s_0,\alpha)]=true$.

Now, if S is blocked for α , at least one of the outermost parallel statements in S , say T' , must be blocked for α , and $D_1(T') \wedge D_2(T') \wedge D_3(T')[value(s_0,\alpha)]=true$. But this is a contradiction, so no such α exists and S cannot be blocked.

5.2.4. Auxiliary Variables.

All of the programs which were shown to be safe from blocking in Sections 5.2.1 and 5.2.3 have included auxiliary variables. The next theorem shows that the programs are also safe from blocking if the auxiliary variables are removed.

5.21. Theorem: Suppose S' is a GPL or RPL program which cannot be blocked, and S is obtained by reduction of S' according to inference rule A8. Then S cannot be blocked.

Proof: Suppose S is blocked for some computation α . By Lemma 3.19 there is a corresponding computation α' for S' which is also blocked. Since this is impossible, S cannot be blocked.

By repeatedly applying Theorem 5.21, all references to auxiliary variables can be deleted, and the resulting program cannot be blocked.

5.3. Termination.

Program termination is an important property for both parallel and sequential programs, although there are correct parallel programs which do not terminate. Various techniques have been suggested for proving termination of sequential programs (Hoare [Ho69], Manna [Ma74]), and the same methods can often be applied to parallel programs. A sequential program can fail to terminate for two reasons: an infinite loop or the execution of an illegal operation such as dividing by zero. With parallel programs there is an additional possibility: the program can be blocked. (It is even possible that a program can be blocked for one computation and loop infinitely for another.) But if a program cannot be blocked, termination can be proved just as it would be for a sequential program.

One approach to proving termination is to show that each statement terminates provided that its primary components terminate. We will not attempt to present general rules for doing this, but will give sufficient conditions for proving that a parallel statement terminates. For similar conditions for sequential statements see Manna [Ma74].

5.22. Definition: T terminates conditionally if it can be proved to terminate under the assumption that it does not become blocked.

5.23 Theorem: If T is a cobegin statement in a GPL or RPL program S which cannot be blocked, and T is not a component of another parallel statement, T terminates if each of its primary components terminates conditionally.

Proof: Suppose T does not terminate. None of its processes can loop indefinitely, so after a finite time each one either finishes or is blocked. At that point T is blocked, and since it is not a proper component of a parallel statement, S is also blocked. Since this is impossible, T must terminate.

Example: Consider the producer and consumer program in Figure 4.5. We have already proved that it cannot be blocked, so we need only show that the producer and consumer processes terminate conditionally. Assuming that the operations required to compute g(A[i]) do not stop execution, the producer must either become blocked or perform M iterations of the loop and terminate. So the producer process terminates conditionally, and the consumer process is similar. By Theorem 5.23 the statement par f g, and thus program fg3 , must terminate.

Note that in this example the producer can be blocked at "add" when count=N . However, it cannot be blocked there forever, since the consumer is not blocked and will eventially remove a unit from the buffer. In general conditional termination implies termination if a process can only be blocked temporarily, as is the case here.

This concludes the discussion of correctness proofs which include properties besides partial correctness. There are many other properties which could be considered: priority assignments, progress for each process, blocking of some subset of the processes in a program, etc. Many of these properties are difficult to define in a uniform way, while others require a model in which there are definite rules for scheduling competing processes. Hopefully, future work will broaden the range of properties which can be proved with axiomatic methods.

CHAPTER 6

CONSISTENCY AND COMPLETENESS OF THE DEDUCTIVE SYSTEM

Throughout this thesis two different methods have been used to describe the semantics of a programming language. The deductive system, consisting of axioms and inference rules, is convenient for proving that a program performs correctly. The interpreter is a model of the way statements are executed on a real machine, and provides considerably more detail than the deductive system. In this chapter we discuss the relationship between these two methods. Either one could be taken as the primary definition of the semantics of the languages. Here we have chosen the interpreter as the basic definition, since it is closer to our intuitive understanding of what parallel programs "mean". From this point of view the consistency theorems in Chapters 2, 3, and 4 state that the deductive system is correct, in the sense that it accurately describes the results of program execution. Section 6.1 is devoted to rather lengthy proofs of these three theorems. Their meaning could be summarized as "anything which can be proved is true".

The converse of consistency is completeness, or "anything which is true can be proved". The axioms and inference rules give significantly less detail about program execution than the interpreter. If the deductive system is complete with respect to the interpreter, we are justified in saying that no essential information is lost by using the axioms. Section 6.2 considers the completeness of the deductive

system for RPL. We will show that the axioms and inference rules given so far are complete in a special sense defined by Cook.

6.1. Consistency.

In this section we will give proofs for Theorems 2.15, 3.15, and 4.18, thus establishing the consistency of the deductive systems and the interpreters for SL, GPL, and RPL. The proofs follow the same pattern in all three cases.

Sequential Language.

The proof of Theorem 2.15 (and also of the other consistency theorems) requires a rather tedious analysis of computations and program states. A few preliminary definitions and lemmas are necessary. The following definition gives a characterization of successor(S), the statement which is next to be executed after S finishes.

6.1. Definition: If S' is a component of an SL program S and a primary component of the statement T , then

successor(S') = T   if T = while B do S'

= T'   if T = begin ... S'; T' ... end

= successor(T)   if T = if B then S' else T'

if B then T' else S'

begin ... S' end

If S' = S , i.e., S' is not a primary component of any T , S has no successor.

6.2. Lemma: If α is a computation for an SL program S , and α finishes S' , then successor(S') is current after α .

Proof: This amounts to showing that program flow in the interpreter follows the usual pattern. Use structural induction, starting with S' = S . In this case, α executes S , and no statement is current after α , just as S has no successor.

Now if S' is a primary component of some statement T , consider the cases in the definition of successor(S') . In the first two cases, next(s,T) creates a control tree in which S' is a son of successor(S') . Thus, when S' is finished, successor(S') is a leaf in the control tree and is current. In the last case, when α finishes S' it finishes T , and by induction successor(S') = successor(T) is current after α .

The next lemma will be used to show that pre(S) and post(S) hold at appropriate times during program execution.

6.3. Lemma: Suppose pre and post are assertion functions for {P} S {Q} , and T is an assign, null, or while statement in S . If α is a computation for S which finishes T , and post(T) is true after α , then

1) if α finishes S' , post(S') is true after α ;

2) if S' is current after α , pre(S') is true after α .

Proof: The proof of this lemma relies on the consistency of the deductive system for the data types of the program (this was discussed in Chapter 2, in connection with the rule of consequence). This consistency implies that if $P \vdash Q$ and P is true, then Q is also true.

<u>Proof of 1)</u>: Induction on the structure of S' . If S' is an assign, null or <u>while</u> statement, S' = T and 1) is true by assumption. If S' = <u>begin</u> ... S_n <u>end</u> , α must finish S_n , and by induction post(S_n) is true after α . Since post(S_n) ⊢ post(S') , post(S') is true after α . If S' is <u>if</u> B <u>then</u> S_1 <u>else</u> S_2 , α finishes either S_1 or S_2 . In either case, post(S_i) is true after α , and post(S_i) ⊢ post(S') , so post(S') is true after α .

<u>Proof of 2)</u>: By Lemma 6.2, S' = successor(T) . Considering Definition 6.1, either S' = <u>while</u> B <u>do</u> T' , or S' follows T' in a sequence of statements. In either case, α finishes T' , making post(T') true after α , and post(T') ⊢ pre(S') . Thus, pre(S') is true after α .

<u>6.4 (2.15) Theorem</u>: If pre and post are assertion functions for {P} S {Q} , S' a component of S , and α a computation for S from a state s_0 satisfying pre(S) , then 1) if S' is ready to execute after α , pre(S') is true after α ; and 2) if α finishes S' , post(S') is true after α .

<u>Proof</u>: Use induction on the length of α . If α is empty, 1) is satisfied because S is current initially and pre(S)[s_0]=true . 2) does not apply.

If α = α'T consider the cases for T .

a) T is x:=E . Then α'T finishes T .

pre(T)[value(s_0,α')]=true by induction

$post(T)^x_E[value(s_0,\alpha')]$=true since $pre(T) \vdash post(T)^x_E$

$post(T)[value(s_0,\alpha)]$=true, since executing $x:=E$ assigns the value of E to x.

By Lemma 6.3, 1) and 2) are satisfied.

b) T = null . By induction $pre(T)[value(s_0,\alpha')]$=true . Now $pre(T) \vdash post(T)$, and T does not change any variables, so $post(T)[value(s_0,\alpha)]$=true. Applying Lemma 6.3 shows that 1) and 2) are satisfied.

c) T is <u>begin</u> $T_1;\ldots;T_n$ <u>end</u> . T is current after α' , so by induction $pre(T)[value(s_0,\alpha')]$=true . Then, $pre(T)[value(s_0,\alpha)]$=true , since T does not change any variables, and $pre(T_1)[value(s_0,\alpha)]$=true , since $pre(T) \vdash pre(T_1)$. Thus 1) is satisfied, and 2) does not apply.

d) T is <u>if</u> B <u>then</u> T_1 <u>else</u> T_2 . By induction $pre(T)[value(s_0,\alpha')]$ =true . If $B[value(s_0,\alpha')]$=true , T_1 is current after $\alpha'T$. Also, $(pre(T) \wedge B)[value(s_0,\alpha'T)]$=true , giving $pre(T_1)[value(s_0,\alpha)]$ =true . If $\neg B[value(s_0,\alpha')]$=true , T_2 is current after $\alpha'T$ and $pre(T_2)[value(s_0,\alpha)]$=true . Thus 1) holds and 2) does not apply.

e) T is <u>while</u> B <u>do</u> T_1 and $B[value(s_0,\alpha')]$=true . This is handled in the same way as case d).

f) T is <u>while</u> B <u>do</u> T_1 and $B[value(s_0,\alpha')]$=false. Then $\alpha = \alpha'T$ finishes T , and $post(T)[value(s_0,\alpha)]$=true since $(pre(T) \wedge \neg B) \vdash post(T)$. Then by Lemma 6.3, 1) and 2) are satisfied.

6.5. (2.16) Corollary: If {P} S {Q} can be proved, it is true in the interpretive model.

Proof: Given in Chapter 2. This is the basic consistency result for sequential programs.

The following corollary will be useful in the discussion of GPL programs.

6.6. Corollary: If S' is current in program state s , and pre(S')[s]=true , then post(S')[execute(s,S')]=true .

Proof: Recall from Definition 2.13 that execute(s,S')=value(s,α) , where α executes S' . Applying Corollary 6.5 yields post(S')·[value(s,α)]=true .

The General Parallel Language.

Next, we prove the consistency of the deductive system for GPL. The first step is to generalize the definitions and lemmas of the last section to include await and parallel statements.

6.7. Definition: If S' is a component of a GPL program S , and a primary component of T ,

successor(S') = successor(T) if T = await B then S' or
cobegin ... //S'// ... coend
= successor(S') from Definition 6.1 otherwise.

6.8. Lemma: If α is a computation for a GPL program S , α finishes S' , and a statement from the same process as S' is current after α , then that statement is successor(S') .

Proof: Essentially the same as Lemma 6.2. There are two new cases for T , where S' is a primary component of T . If T is a parallel statement, finishing S' will not necessarily finish T , since other processes of T may still be in execution. In this case, however, no statement from the same process as S' is current. If α finishes T , by induction successor(T) = successor(S) is current in α .

If T is await B then S' , the interpreter executes T indivisibly, and S' never appears in a computation. So this case does not occur.

6.9. Lemma: Suppose pre and post are assertion functions for {P} S {Q} , and α is a computation for S which finishes T , where T is an assign, null, while, or await statement. If post(T) holds after α , and S' and T are from the same process, then

1) if α finishes S' , post(S') is true after α .

2) if S' is current after α , pre(S') is true after α .

Proof: 1) The same as Lemma 6.3, with two new cases for S' . If S' = await..., then S' = T and 1) is true. If S' = cobegin S_1 //...// S_n coend and α finishes S' , α finishes each S_i . By induction, $(\bigwedge_i \text{post}(S_i))$ is true after α , and since $(\bigwedge_i \text{post}(S_i)) \vdash \text{post}(S')$, post(S') is true after α .

2) Same as Lemma 6.3.

<u>6.10. (3.15) Theorem</u>: If S is a GPL program with assertion functions pre and post for {P} S {Q} , S' is a component of S and α a computation for S from s_0 with $P[s_0]$=true , then

1) if S' is current after α , pre(S') holds after α ;

2) if α finishes S' , post(S') holds after α .

<u>Proof</u>: By induction on the length of α . If α is empty, pre(S)[value(s_0,α)]=pre(S)[s_0]=true by assumption, and no other statement is current after α . Also α does not finish any statement, so 2) does not apply. If $\alpha = \alpha'T$, there are two cases to consider.

<u>Case 1</u>: S' and T are from the same process. This is just the same as the sequential problem. It is only necessary to consider the two new cases of T .

g) T = <u>cobegin</u> T_1 //...// T_n <u>coend</u> . Then each T_i is current after $\alpha'T$, and since pre(T) $\vdash (\bigwedge_i \text{pre}(T_i))$, pre($T_i$)[value($s_0$,$\alpha$)]=true. This makes 1) hold, and 2) does not apply.

h) T is <u>await</u> B <u>then</u> T_1 . By induction and the fact that T is ready to execute after α' , (pre(T) $\wedge$ B)[value(s_0,α')]=true , and pre(T_1)[value(s_0,α')]=true , since pre(T) $\wedge$ B $\vdash$ pre(T_1) . Now value(s_0,$\alpha'T$)=execute(value(s_0,α), T_1) , and by Corollary 6.6, post(T_1)[value(s_0,α)]=true . But then post(T)[value(s_0,α)]=true , since post(T_1) $\vdash$ post(T) . Applying Lemma 6.9 shows that 1) and 2) hold.

<u>Case 2</u>: S' and T are from different processes. Note that if S' is current after $\alpha'T$, S' is current for α' and by induction

$pre(S')[value(s_0,\alpha')]=true$. If T is a null, _if_, _begin_, _while_, or parallel statement, the variables have the same value in $\alpha'T$ as in α', so $pre(S')[value(s_0,\alpha)]=true$. If T is an assignment or _await_ statement, $\{pre(T) \wedge pre(S')\}$ T $\{pre(S')\}$ can be proved (this is the interference-free property). Now by induction, $(pre(T) \wedge pre(S'))\cdot [value(s_0,\alpha')]=true$, so $pre(S')[value(s_0,\alpha'T)]=true$.

If $\alpha'T$ finishes S' , α' also finishes S' , and by induction $post(S')[value(s_0,\alpha')]=true$. Once again the interference-free property guarantees that $post(S')[value(s_0,\alpha'T)]=true$. Thus 1) and 2) hold in case 2.

6.11. (3.16) Corollary (consistency of A0-A7 for GPL): If S is a GPL program and {P} S {Q} can be proved, it is true in the interpretive model.

Proof: In Chapter 3.

6.12. (3.20) Theorem (consistency of A8 for GPL): If S' is a GPL program and S is a reduction of S' which satisfies the auxiliary variable rule, then {P} S {Q} is true in the model.

Proof: In Chapter 3.

The Restricted Parallel Language.

Consistency for the RPL deductive system can be proved in much the same way as for GPL.

6.13. Definition: If S' is a component of an RPL program S , and a primary component of T ,

successor(S') = successor(T) if T is resource $r_1,\ldots,r_m$:
cobegin ... //S'// ... coend
or with r when B do S'
= successor(S') from Definition 6.1 otherwise.

6.14. Lemma: If α is a computation for a GPL program S which finishes S' , and a statement from the same process as S' is current after α , then that statement is successor(S') .

Proof: As in Lemma 6.8, consider the cases for T , where S' is a primary component of T . If T is one of the five sequential statements, or a cobegin statement, the proof is the same as Lemma 6.8. If T is with r when B do S' , α finishes S' , and by induction successor(S') = successor(T) is current after α .

6.15. Lemma: Suppose pre, post, and I are assertion functions for {P} S {Q} and T is an assignment, null, or while statement in S . If α = α'T is a computation for S which finishes T , and post(T) holds after α , then

1) if α finishes S' , post(S') holds after α ;

2) if S' is current after α , pre(S') holds after α .

Proof: 1) Consider the cases for S' . If S' is assign, null, while, begin, if, or cobegin the argument is the same as for Lemma 6.9.

If S' is <u>with</u> r <u>when</u> B <u>do</u> S_1 , α finishes S_1 , and by induction $post(S_1)$ holds after α . Since $post(S_1) \vdash post(S')$, $post(S')$ holds after α .

2) Same as for Lemma 6.9.

<u>6.16. (4.18) Theorem</u>: Suppose S is an RPL program, and pre, post, and I are assertion functions for $\{P\}$ S $\{Q\}$. If α is a computation for S from state s_0 with $P[s_0]$=true , then

1) if S' is current after α , $pre(S')$ holds after α ;

2) if α finishes S' , $post(S')$ holds after α ;

3) if resource r is declared in a statement which is in execution for α , and r is not busy for α , $I(r)$ holds after α .

<u>Proof</u>: By induction on the length of α .

If α is empty, $pre(S)[value(s_0,\alpha)]$=true by assumption, and no other statement is current in α , so 1) holds. α does not finish any statements, so 2) does not apply. If 3) applies, S must be a parallel statement in which r is declared, and 3) holds because $pre(S) \vdash I(r)$.

If $\alpha = \alpha' T$, we first show that 1) and 2) are satisfied. Consider two cases:

<u>Case 1</u>: S' and T are from the same process. This is the same as case 1 of Theorem 6.10 if T is <u>cobegin</u> or one of the five sequential statements. The other possibility is that T is <u>with</u> r <u>when</u> B <u>do</u> T' . After α , T' is current. Since T is ready to execute after α' , r is not busy for α' , and by induction $I(r)[value(s_0,\alpha')]$=true .

Also $B[\text{value}(s_0,\alpha')]=\text{true}$, and by induction $\text{pre}(T)[\text{value}(s_0,\alpha')]=\text{true}$. Then $\text{pre}(T_1)[\text{value}(s_0,\alpha)]=\text{true}$, since $(\text{pre}(T) \wedge B \wedge I(r)) \vdash \text{pre}(T_1)$, and starting T does not modify any variable values. So 1) holds, and 2) does not apply.

Case 2: S' and T are from different processes. Note that if S' is current for $\alpha'T$ (or $\alpha'T$ finishes S'), S' is current for α' (or α' finishes S') and by induction $\text{pre}(S')[\text{value}(s_0,\alpha')]=\text{true}$ (or $\text{post}(S')[\text{value}(s_0,\alpha')]=\text{true}$). By Lemma 4.14, T does not change a variable in Proof-var(S') , so $\text{pre}(S')[\text{value}(s_0,\alpha)]=\text{true}$ (or $\text{post}(S')[\text{value}(s_0,\alpha)]=\text{true}$).

Finally, we must show that 3) holds. Let T' be the parallel statement in which r was declared. If T' is not in execution for $\alpha'T$, 3) does not apply, so assume T' is in execution for $\alpha'T$. If T' is current for α , $\text{pre}(T')[\text{value}(s_0,\alpha)]=\text{true}$ and $I(r)\cdot[\text{value}(s_0,\alpha)]=\text{true}$ since $\text{pre}(T') \vdash I(r)$. If not, T' is in execution for α' , and by induction, 3) is satisfied for α' . There are two ways in which $\alpha'T$ could fail to satisfy 3).

a) T changes a variable which is free in I(r) . But in this case r is busy in $\alpha'T$, so I(r) does not have to be true.

b) $\alpha'T$ finishes a critical section for r , i.e., T makes r not busy. But then from case 1 above, $I(r)[\text{value}(s_0,\alpha)]=\text{true}$.

6.17. (4.20) Corollary (consistency for RPL): If S is an RPL program and {P} S {Q} can be proved, it is true in the interpretive model.

Proof: In Chapter 4.

The consistency results of this section imply that if $\{P\}\ S\ \{Q\}$ can be proved, it is true for the interpreter. If the interpreter is a good model of parallel execution on a real machine, then the deductive system is also valid for real machines.

There are several ways in which a real implementation might differ from the interpreter. The most fundamental is that the interpreter does not allow true parallel execution, but simulates it by nondeterminism. In this respect it is a model of multiprogramming, but not of multiprocessing. In Chapter 3 and 4 we have argued that the languages GPL and RPL are defined in a way which guarantees that nondeterminism and parallelism give the same results for all programs.

A second possible difference is in the treatment of expressions which are normally considered to be undefined, such as those involving division by zero; this was discussed in Chapter 2. The interpreter gives these expressions an arbitrary value, but it would also be reasonable to stop execution as soon as such an expression was encountered. The axioms and inference rules are also consistent with this treatment of the problem, since any formula $\{P\}\ S\ \{Q\}$ is true if S does not terminate.

A third area in which a particular implementation might differ from the interpreter is by specifying in more detail the way parallel processes are scheduled. For example, processes which are competing for a resource might be guaranteed to receive it on a first-come, first-served basis. Such an implementation is consistent with the interpreter, so it is also consistent with the axioms and inference rules.

All of this suggests that the deductive system accurately describes the behavior of parallel programs when executed on a real machine. To prove that this is true for any particular machine requires a proof that the implementation of the language on that machine is correct with respect to the semantics defined by the interpreter. Such a proof would be a major undertaking, but a similar result has been obtained for the implementation of a sequential language [Mi72].

6.2. Completeness.

The last section established the consistency of the deductive system and the interpreter; now we would like to show that the deductive system is also complete with respect to the interpreter. Unfortunately we cannot hope to do this in general, as the following example shows.

If the programming language SL operates on data types which include the natural numbers and the standard operations on them, it can be used to encode a Turing machine. Let S be a program which encodes a Turing machine that does not halt on any input; then S does not terminate from any initial state. For such a program {true} S {false} is trivially true. The set of Turing machines which do not halt on any input is not recursively enumerable, but the set of provable formulas is, so in general {true} S {false} cannot be proved.

Although the deductive system cannot be complete for any programming language which includes the integers, this does not necessarily mean that the axioms and inference rules are inadequate for describing the programming language. Part of the problem is the fact that there is no complete first-order deductive system for the natural numbers. Recall the form of A0 (the rule of consequence).

$$\text{A0: } \frac{\{P'\}\ S\ \{Q'\},\ P \vdash P',\ Q' \vdash Q}{\{P\}\ S\ \{Q\}}$$

In order to use this rule, it is necessary to prove P' from P and Q from Q', using some deductive system D for the data types of the programming language. When we presented A0 in Chapter 2, we made no assumptions about the choice of D except that it is consistent with the data types of the language. D cannot be complete if the data types include the natural numbers, by the Gödel incompleteness theorem, so the incompleteness of the deductive system for programming languages is not surprising. Now suppose D' is some complete proof system for the data types of the language (in general D' will not be effective). If using D' in A0 yields a complete proof system for the programming language, we will say that the original deductive system is <u>relatively complete</u>. Relative completeness suggests that the axioms and inference rules give "enough" information about program execution, and that the incompleteness of the deductive system is due to the incompleteness of D. This approach is due to Cook [Co75], who used it to prove the relative completeness of a deductive system for a sequential language.

In this chapter we give a proof of the relative completeness of A0-A8 for RPL programs with a wide class of data domains. (The rules for GPL and SL are also relatively complete, but that will not be proved here.) As a first step we prove relative completeness for programs in a language which contains the natural numbers with $<,=,+,*,$ and $||$ (concatenation, to be defined shortly). The language L used for assertions in a program proof will be the first-order predicate calculus language whose nonlogical symbols are $\{<,=,+,*,||,0,1,\ldots\}$.

Concatenation is an operation which is useful for representing sequences of natural numbers: it is included in the programming language operations because it will be necessary to introduce auxiliary variables which store sequences.

<u>6.18. Definition</u>: The operation of <u>concatenation</u>, written $x||y$, is defined by

$$
\begin{aligned}
x||y &= 10*x + 2 \text{ , if } y = 0 \\
&= (10*x + 1)||(y-1) \text{ , otherwise}
\end{aligned}
$$

A finite sequence $n_1,n_2,\ldots,n_k$ can be represented by the integer $(\ldots((0||n_1)||n_2)\ldots)||n_k$. Here each number n_i in the sequence is represented as n_i 1's followed by a 2. For example, the sequence 2,0,4 is expressed as

$$((0||2)||0)||4 = 112211112 .$$

Note that 0 represents the null sequence.

<u>6.19. Theorem (Relative completeness of RPL)</u>: Let T be a program in a version of RPL whose data domain is the natural numbers with $<,=,+,*,$ and $||$.

Let D' be a complete proof system for the natural numbers (D' will not be effective). Then if {P} T {Q} is true in the interpretive model, it can be proved using D' and A0-A8.

Proof: Sections 6.2.1-6.2.3 are devoted to a proof of this theorem for the case in which T contains at most one cobegin statement. If T contains more than one cobegin the principle is the same, although the details are more complicated. The approach used in the proof is outlined below:

6.2.1. Construct a program T* by adding auxiliary variables to T. Show that {P} T* {Q} is true in the interpretive model.

6.2.2. Define pre, post, and I for T*.

6.2.3. Show that pre, post, and I are assertion functions for {P} T* {Q}, which implies that {P} T* {Q} can be proved. Then A8 can be applied to remove auxiliary variables, giving a proof of {P} T {Q}.

The crux of the proof is defining assertion functions pre(S), post(S), and I(r) which depend only on the variables in Proof-var(S) and Proof-var(r), respectively. In program T, which contains a single cobegin statement T_0 =

$$L_0\text{: } \underline{\text{resource}}\ r_1,\ldots,r_M\text{: } \underline{\text{cobegin}}\ L_1\text{: } T_1\ //\ldots//\ L_N\text{: } T_N\ \underline{\text{coend}}$$

Proof-var(r_j) = {x: x is not assigned a value in T_0 except in a withwhen statement for r_j}

Proof-var(S) = {variables of T} if S is not a proper component of T_0

$$\text{Proof-var}(T_k) = \{x\text{: no statement of } T_j \text{ , } j \neq k \text{ , assigns a value to } x\}$$

$$\text{Proof-var}(S) = \text{Proof-var}(T_k) \cup \Big(\bigcup_{\substack{S \text{ a proper component} \\ \text{of a \underline{withwhen} for } r}} \text{Proof-var}(r) \Big)$$

The details of the proof depend heavily on the operation of the RPL interpreter, and the reader may wish to review Section 4.2, especially Definition 4.4 to 4.10.

Section 6.2.4 considers the implications of the relative completeness theorem, and shows how it can be broadened to apply to the standard programming language data types.

6.2.1. The Program T* .

In this section we will define a program T* by adding auxiliary variables to T . Before describing the general construction for T* , however, we present a simple example which illustrates the techniques involved.

An Example -- The Program AorB.

Consider the program AorB in Figure 6.1. For this program {true} AorB {Afirst=1 V Bfirst=1} is true in the interpretive model, because any computation must execute A1 before B2, setting Afirst=1 , or B1 before A2, setting Bfirst=1 . This is illustrated in Figure 6.1 by listing several computations and the final variables values in each case. Note that not all computations are included, since A1 and BI, as well as A2 and B2, can be executed in parallel. Since A1 and B1 have no variables in common, the results are the same whether A1

```
AorB: begin doneA1:=doneB1:=0;
          resource r1(doneA1), r2(doneB1): cobegin
            A: begin
               A1: with r1 do doneA1:=1;
               A2: with r2 do Bfirst:=doneB1;
               end
          //
            B: begin
               B1: with r2 do doneB1:=1;
               B2: with r1 do Afirst:=doneA1;
               end
          coend
      end
```

	Computation	Final Values Afirst	Final Values Bfirst
1.	A1 A2 B1 B2	1	0
2.	A1 B1 A2 B2	1	1
3.	A1 B1 B2 A2	1	1
4.	B1 A1 A2 B2	1	1
5.	B1 A1 B2 A2	1	1
6.	B1 B2 A1 A2	0	1

Figure 6.1. Program AorB and Several Computations.

precedes B1, or B1 precedes A1, or their execution overlaps. The same is true for A2 and B2, so the 6 possibilities in Figure 6.1 represent all of the interesting cases.

In order to prove {true} AorB {Afirst=1 V Bfirst=1} , it is necessary to add auxiliary variables to AorB. Figure 6.2 shows the augmented program AorB' and Figure 6.3 gives the final variable values for the six computations of Figure 6.1. Note that the final values of the variables A1time , A2time , B1time , B2time make it possible to reconstruct the order in which statements were executed. The rule is that if xtime<ytime , statement x was executed before statement y . If xtime=ytime , the two statements were executed at about the same time, with the exact order irrelevant. In the first computation, for example, we can tell that A1 was the first statement executed, and it was followed by A2, B1, and B2 in that order. For the second computation, the final values show that A1 was executed before A2 and B2, and that B1 preceded A2 and B2. We cannot tell whether or not A1 preceded B1, or A2 preceded B2, but this is unimportant because the final variable values are the same in any case.

Figure 6.4 gives some assertions for {true} AorB'{Afirst=1 V Bfirst=1} . The reader can verify that they are correct. This is quite straightforward except for showing that (post(A) ∧ post(B) ∧ I(r1) ∧ I(r2)) $\vdash$ (Afirst=1 V Bfirst=1) . To verify this, assume (post(A) ∧ post(B) ∧ I(r1) ∧ I(r2)) . This implies:

1. A2time>A1time ∧ B2time>B1time
2. A1time≠B2time ∧ B1time≠A2time

```
AorB': begin
   Atime:=Btime:=r1time:=r2time:=0;
   A1time:=A2time:=B1time:=B2time:=0;
   doneA1:=doneB1:=0;
   resource r1(doneA1,r1time),r2(doneB1,r2time):
        cobegin
           A: begin
              A1: with r1 do
                    begin A1time:=1+max(Atime,r1time);
                          Atime:=r1time:=A1time;
                          doneA1:=1
                    end
              A2: with r2 do
                    begin A2time:=1+max(Atime,r2time);
                          Atime:=r2time:=A2time;
                          Bfirst:=doneB1
                    end
              end
        //
           B: begin
              B1: with r2 do
                    begin B1time:=1+max(Btime,r2time);
                          Btime:=r2time:=B1time;
                          doneB1:=1
                    end
              B2: with r1 do
                    begin B2time:=1+max(Btime,r1time);
                          Btime:=r1time:=B2time;
                          Afirst:=doneA1
                    end
              end
        coend
   end
```

Figure 6.2. Program AorB'.

		Final Values					
	Computation	Afirst	Bfirst	A1time	A2time	B1time	B2time
1.	A1 A2 B1 B2	1	0	1	2	3	4
2.	A1 B1 A2 B2	1	1	1	2	1	2
3.	A1 B1 B2 A2	1	1	1	2	1	2
4.	B1 A1 A2 B2	1	1	1	2	1	2
5.	B1 A1 B2 A2	1	1	1	2	1	2
6.	B1 B2 A1 A2	0	1	3	4	1	2

Figure 6.3. Final Values for Computations of AorB'.

```
{true} begin
      Atime:=Btime:=r1time:=r2time:=A1time:=A2time:=B1time:=B2time:=0;
      doneA1:=doneB1:=0;
      {all variables have the value 0}
      resource r1(doneA1,r1time), r2(doneB1,r2time): cobegin
         A: {A1time=A2time=Atime=0}
            begin A1: with r1 do
                        begin A1time:=1+max(Atime,r1time);
                              Atime:=r1time:=A1time;
                              doneA1:=1
                        end
                   {A2time=0 ∧ Atime=A1time>0}
                   A2: with r2 do
                        begin A2time:=1+max(Atime,r2time);
                              Atime:=r2time:=A2time;
                              Bfirst:=doneB1;
                        end
                   {A2time=Atime>A1time>0}
            end
         {A2time>A1time>0}
      //
         {B1time=B2time=Btime=0} B {B2time>B1time>0}
            (processes A and B are symmetric)
      coend
      {Afirst=1 ∨ Bfirst=1}
end
{Afirst=1 ∨ Bfirst=1}


I(r1) = {(A1time>0 ⇒ doneA1=1) ∧ (r1time≥A1time ∧ r1time≥B2time) ∧
         (A1time=B2time ⇒ both are 0) ∧ (B2time>A1time>0 ⇒ Afirst=1)}
I(r2) = {(B1time>0 ⇒ doneB1=1) ∧ (r2time≥B1time ∧ r2time≥A2time)
         (A2time=B1time ⇒ both are 0) ∧ (A2time>B1time>0 ⇒ Bfirst=1)}
```

Figure 6.4. Informal Proof of {true}AorB'{Afirst=1 ∨ Bfirst=1}.

3. B2time>A1time ⇒ Afirst=1

4. A2time>B1time ⇒ Bfirst=1

Assume Afirst≠1 . Then from 3 and 2, A1time>B2time ; from 1, A2time>B1time ; and from 4, Bfirst=1 . Thus,

$$(\text{post}(A) \land \text{post}(B) \land I(r1) \land I(r2)) \vdash (\text{Afirst}=1 \lor \text{Bfirst}=1) .$$

The use of variables in the proof is legitimate, since

Proof-var(A) = {doneA1,Bfirst,Atime,A1time,A2time}

Proof-var(B) = {doneB1,Afirst,Btime,B1time,B2time}

Proof-var(r1) = {doneA1,Afirst,r1time,A1time,B2time}

Proof-var(r2) = {doneB1,Bfirst,r2time,B1time,A2time}

The auxiliary variables A1time ... B2time are particularly useful because each belongs to the proof-variables of a process and a resource. Thus A1time , for example, can be used in pre and post assertions for statements in process A , as well as in I(r1) . Since the "time" variables encode enough information to determine the order of statement execution, they make it possible to prove that if A1 did not precede B2, B1 must have preceded A2.

The Definition of T*.

The construction of an augmented program T* for an arbitrary program T containing at most one <u>cobegin</u> statement is accomplished by adding two kinds of auxiliary variables to T . The first type are "time" variables, like those in AorB' ; the second are "history" variables, used to record the values of program variables at key points during program execution.

<u>6.20. Definition</u>: Recall that program T of Theorem 6.19 has at most one <u>cobegin</u> statement T_0 =

L_0: <u>resource</u> $r_1,\ldots,r_M$: <u>cobegin</u> L_1: T_1 //...// L_N: T_N <u>coend</u> .

Let S be any component of T . Then

<u>resources(S)</u> = $\{r_j$: S is a proper component of a <u>withwhen</u> statement for $r_j\}$

<u>var(S)</u> = {variables of T}, if S is not a proper component of T_0

= {x: x does not appear on the left side of an assignment statement in T_i , $i \neq k\}$, if $S = T_k$

$= \mathrm{var}(T_k) \cup (\bigcup_{r \in \mathrm{resources}(S)} r)$, if S is a proper component of T_k

Note that var(S) is the set of variables which may legally be used in S , according to Definition 4.3.

<u>6.21. Definition</u>: The auxiliary variables to be added to the program T of Theorem 6.19 are defined as follows. If T contains no parallel statement then T requires no auxiliary variables. If T contains the parallel statement T_0 =

L_0: <u>resource</u> $r_1,\ldots,r_M$: <u>cobegin</u> L_1: T_1 //...// L_N: T_N <u>coend</u> ,

the auxiliary variables are:

1. L_1time,...,$L_N$time - used like Atime and Btime in the program AorB'
2. $r_1$time,...,$r_M$time -- used like $r_1$time and $r_2$time in AorB'
3. for each variable x in T , L_0initial x -- records the value of x at the beginning of statement L_0
4. for each statement in process T_k with the form L: with r_j when B do S_1 , and each variables $x \in var(S_1) \cup \{L_k time, r_j time\}$, L history x -- records the sequence of values of x at the beginning of each execution of L .

Of course it is assumed that none of these variables occur in the original program. If this is not true, some variables must be renamed.

6.22. Definition: The program T* required in the proof of {P} T {Q} is obtained by adding auxiliary variables to T as described below:

1. if T contains no cobegin statement, T*=T
2. otherwise replace the cobegin statement

   L_0: resource r_1,...,r_M: cobegin L_1: T_1 //...// L_N: T_N coend

   by

```
begin r1time:=r2time:=...:=rMtime:=0;
      L1time:=L2time:=...:=LNtime:=0;
      L history x:=0; (for each  L history x  of Definition 6.21)
      L0initial x:=x; (for each  x ε var(T))
      resource r1(...,r1time),...,rM(...,rMtime):
         cobegin L1: T1* //...// LN: TN* coend
end
```

Here T_k* is the result of adding auxiliary variables to T_k.

Next, replace each statement L: <u>with</u> r_j <u>when</u> B <u>do</u> S_1 in process T_k by

```
begin L_k time:=1+max(L_k time,r_j time);
        L history x := L history x || x; (for each  x ε var(S_1*))
        S_1*;
        r_j time:=L_k time;
end
```

Here S_1* is the result of adding auxiliary variables to S_1.

The time variables are used as they were in AorB' to give information about the order in which critical sections are executed. Setting $L_k$time=1+max($L_k$time,$r_j$time) records the fact that L was started after any critical section which has already been started in process T_k and after any other critical section for r_j which has already been executed. Because S_1 may contain a <u>withwhen</u> statement for another resource, $L_k$time is updated before starting S_1*. Since no other <u>withwhen</u> for r_j can be started until L is finished, $r_j$time is updated after S_1*, just before releasing control of r_j.

The L history and L_0initial variables are used to record variable values at key points. L_0initial x is the value x had when the most recent execution of the <u>cobegin</u> statement L_0 began. L history x contains the sequence of values assumed by x at the beginning of each execution of statement L (in the most recent execution of L_0). The purpose of introducing these variables will become clear as the proof proceeds. For now, note that part of their usefulness stems from the variety of assertions in which they can appear:

L_0initial x belongs to Proof-var(L_k) , $1 \le k \le N$, and Proof-var(r_j) , $1 \le j \le M$, since it is not modified at all inside the <u>cobegin</u> statement T_0 .

L history x , where L is a <u>withwhen</u> statement for resource r_j in process T_k , belongs to Proof-var(T_k) and Proof-var(r_j) since it is changed only inside the statement L .

The variables added in creating T* are auxiliary variables, as they satisfy Definition 3.17. This means that {P} T {Q} can be proved by first proving {P} T* {Q} and then using A8 to remove the added statements. The following theorem shows that {P} T* {Q} is true for the interpretive model.

<u>6.23. Theorem</u>: Let AV be an auxiliary variable set for an RPL program S' , S be a reduction of S' with respect to AV , and P' and Q' be assertions which do not contain free any variables from AV . Then if {P'} S {Q'} is true for the interpreter, so is {P'} S' {Q'} .

<u>Proof</u>: This is the converse of Theorem 4.19, and the proof is very similar. We must show that if $P'[s_0]$=true and α' executes S' then $Q'[\text{value}(s_0,\alpha')]$=true . Given α' which executes S' , let α be a computation for S which is like α' except that the statement removed from S' is removed from α' . Now α and α' have the same flow of control and the same effect on the variables in P' and Q'

(see Lemma 3.19). Then $P'[s_0]=\text{true} \Rightarrow Q'[\text{value}(s_0,\alpha)]=\text{true}$ (because {P'} S' {Q'} is true in the model), and thus $Q'[\text{value}(s_0,\alpha')]=\text{true}$. So {P'} S {Q'} is true in the interpretive model.

<u>6.24. Corollary</u>: {P} T* {Q} is true in the interpretive model.

<u>Proof</u>: {P} T {Q} is true for the interpreter, and T can be obtained from T* by repeated reduction steps.

<u>6.2.2. The Functions pre, post, and I for T* .</u>

Having constructed the program T* , our next step will be to define assertion functions for {P} T* {Q} . First let us consider a statement S which is not a proper component of the <u>cobegin</u> statement.

<u>6.25. Definition</u>: Let S be a component of T* , but not a proper component of a <u>cobegin</u> statement. The predicates pre'(S) and post'(S) defined on program states are

pre'(S)(s) ≡ ∃ a program state s_0 and a computation α for T* such that $P[s_0]=\text{true}$ and S is current after α and $x[s]=x[\text{value}(s_0,\alpha)]\ \forall\ x$.

post'(S)(s) ≡ ∃ a program state s_0 and a computation α for T* such that $P[s_0]=\text{true}$ and α finishes S and $x[s]=x[\text{value}(s_0,\alpha)]\ \forall\ x$.

Informally, pre'(S)(s) is true iff it is possible to start T* with P true and reach S with variables as given by state s .

Post'(S)(s) is true iff it is possible to start T* with P true and finish S with variables as given by state s .

Now pre' and post' as defined above are recursively enumerable predicates, and as such can always be expressed as first-order formulas in the language L whose nonlogical symbols are $\{<,=,+,*,||,0,1,\ldots\}$.

<u>6.26. Definition</u>: For S a component of T* , but not a proper component of a <u>cobegin</u> statement, let <u>pre(S)</u> and <u>post(S)</u> be first-order formulas of L which express the predicates pre'(S) and post'(S), i.e.,

$$\text{pre}(S)[s] \equiv \text{pre}'(S)(s)$$

$$\text{post}(S)[s] \equiv \text{post}'(S)(s) \ .$$

Pre and post as given above satisfy the definition of assertion functions (Definition 4.15). As an example, consider the case where S is the assignment statement y:=E . Part 2 of Definition 4.15 requires that $\text{pre}(S) \vdash \text{post}(S)^y_E$. The first step in verifying this is to show that $\text{pre}(S) \Rightarrow \text{post}(S)^y_E$. Let s be a state with pre(S)[s]=true . Then pre'(S)(s) is true, and

$$\exists\, s_0,\alpha \text{ such that } P[s_0]=\text{true and } S \text{ is current after } \alpha \text{ , and } x[s]=x[\text{value}(s_0,\alpha)]\ \forall\, x \ .$$

Since S is current after α , αS is a computation, and $\text{value}(s_0,\alpha S)= \text{value}(s_0,\alpha)\langle y|E\rangle$. Then αS is a computation which finishes S , and $x[\text{value}(s_0,\alpha S)]=x[\text{value}(s_0,\alpha)\langle y|E\rangle]=x[s\langle y|E\rangle]\ \forall\, x$, giving post'(S)(s<y|E>)=true . Thus, pre(S)[s] $\Rightarrow$ post(S)[s<y|E>] , or pre(S) $\Rightarrow$ post$(S)^y_E$.

Since pre(S) $\Rightarrow$ post$(S)^y_E$ is true for the natural numbers, pre(S) $\vdash$ post$(S)^y_E$ using D' , the complete proof system for the natural numbers of Theorem 6.19.

This definition of pre and post is not acceptable for a statement S which is a proper component of a cobegin statement, for then pre(S) and post(S) can only refer to variables in Proof-var(S) . In order to define pre and post for such statements we need the concept of a local computation for the parallel process containing S . Consider a computation α for the program T* . If β is the subsequence of α consisting of all statements from process T_k , β can be called a local computation for T_k . But where α uniquely determines the final values of the variables in Proof-var(T*) , β does not determine the values of variables in Proof-var(T_k) , because these may depend on the values of resource variables which are changed unpredictably by other processes. For this reason a local computation cannot be just a sequence of statements, but must be a sequence of statements and program states. More formally:

6.27. Definition: Let T_k be one of the parallel processes in program T . A local computation β for T_k is a sequence $s_0\ (S_1,s_1)\ \ldots\ (S_n,s_n)$, $0\le n$, where s_i is a program state, $0\le i\le n$, S_i is a component of T_k , $1\le i\le n$, and

1. the control state of s_0 contains the single node T_k

2. for $1 \leq i \leq n$

   a. S_i is current in s_{i-1}

   b. if S_i is <u>with</u> r <u>when</u> B <u>do</u> S , $B[s_i]$=true

   c. s_i=next(s_{i-1},S_i) except that if $x \notin var(S_i)$, $x[s_i]$ may take on any value

If β is a local computation, let <u>value(β)=s_n</u> .

Note that a computation and a local computation are very similar. There are 3 main differences.

1. In the local computation, 2c allows the values of nonlocal variables to change arbitrarily, reflecting the fact that other processes may modify their values while T_k is being executed.
2. In a computation for T_k , each state s_i is uniquely defined by s_i=next(s_{i-1},S_i) , so the computation is determined by the initial state and the sequence of statements. In a local computation, s_i is not uniquely determined by s_{i-1} and S_i , so the local computation consists of a sequence of statements and program states.
3. In a computation, S_i must be ready to execute (Definition 4.6) in s_{i-1} . In a local computation 2a and b are similar to "ready to execute", but it is not necessary to require that r is not busy, since we are only considering the execution of a single process.

If α is a computation for T* it is always possible to derive a local computation for process T_k which executes the statements of T_k in the same order as α . But it is not always possible to find a computation for T* consistent with a given local computation for T_k .

This is because Definition 6.27 may allow nonlocal variables to assume values that never could arise in a real computation.

6.28. Definition: A local computation β for T_k is acceptable iff its initial state s_0 has $pre(T_0)[s_0]=true$, where T_0 is the parallel statement of T* . This implies that it is possible to start T* with P true and reach the beginning of T_k in state s_0 .

A local computation contains only statements from one process. A related concept is the resource computation, which contains only statements which operate on a particular resource.

6.29. Definition: A resource computation γ for a resource r_j is a sequence $s_0\ (S_1,s_1)\ \ldots\ (S_n,s_n)$, $0\leq n$, where s_i is a program state, $0\leq i\leq n$, S_i is a component of a withwhen statement for r_j , $1\leq i\leq n$, and

1. the control state of s_0 is empty
2. if S_i is L: with r_j when B do S' , $1\leq i\leq n$
   a. the control of s_{i-1} is empty
   b. the control of s_i is the single node S'
   c. $x[s_i]=x[s_{i-1}]\ \forall\ x\varepsilon r$
3. if S_i is not a withwhen statement for r_j , $1\leq i\leq n$
   a. S_i is current in s_{i-1}
   b. if S_i is with r when B do S , $B[s_i]=true$
   c. $s_i=next(s_{i-1},S_i)$ except that if $x\notin var(S_i)$, $x[s_i]$ may take on any value;

If γ is a resource computation, let value(γ)=s_n .

A resource computation γ for r represents the execution of a sequence of withwhen statements -- the only statements where the variables of r are accessible. It has the form $\gamma = \gamma_1\gamma_2 \cdots \gamma_k$, where γ_i is a subsequence of γ which executes one withwhen statement for r_j . Part 2 of the definition describes what happens when a new withwhen statement L is started, while part 3 (the same as 2a-c for a local computation) describes the remainder of the execution of L . Because of 2a, a new withwhen for r_j cannot be started until the previous one is finished.

If α is a computation for T* , it is always possible to derive a resource computation for r which executes critical sections for r in the same order as α . But it is not always possible to find a computation for T* which is consistent with a particular resource computation, since 2c and 3c allow nonlocal variables to assume arbitrary values.

6.30. Definition: A resource computation γ is acceptable iff its initial state s_0 has $pre(T_0)[s_0]$=true , i.e., it is possible to start T* with P true and reach T_0 in state s_0 .

Now pre(S) , post(S) and I(r) can be defined using local and resource computations. The first step is to define predicates pre'(S) , post'(S) and I'(r) on program states.

6.31. Definition: If S is a component and r a resource of T* , let the predicates pre'(S) , post'(S) , and I'(r) be defined as follows. If S is not a proper component of the cobegin statement

T_0 , pre'(S) and post'(S) are given in Definition 6.25. If S is a component of process T_k ,

pre'(S)(s) ≡ ∃ an acceptable local computation β for T_k with S current after β and x[s]=x[value(β)] ∀ xεProof-var(S) , and ∀ rεresources(S) ∃ an acceptable resource computation γ_r for r with S current after γ_r and x[s]= x[value(γ_r)] ∀ xεProof-var(S) .

post'(S)(s) ≡ ∃ an acceptable local computation β for T_k which finishes S , and x[s]=x[value(β)] ∀ xεProof-var(S) , and ∀ rεresources(S) ∃ an acceptable resource computation γ_r for r which finishes S , and x[s]=x[value(γ_r)] ∀ xεProof-var(S) .

For all resources r_j ,

I'(r_j)(s) ≡ ∃ an acceptable resource computation γ for r , with the control of value(γ) empty, and x[s]=x[value(γ)] ∀ xεProof-var(r) .

These definitions can be informally summarized as:

pre'(S)(s) ≡ The state s is compatible with some local computation which reaches S . If S is a proper component of a withwhen statement for r , s is also compatible with some resource computation for r which reaches S .

post'(S)(s) ≡ The state s is compatible with some local computation which finishes S . If S is a proper component of a withwhen statement for r , s is also compatible with some resource computation for r which finishes S .

I'(r)(s) ≡ The state s is compatible with some resource computation which is not in the midst of executing a critical section for r .

Since pre'(S) , post'(S) , and I'(r) are recursively enumerable predicates, they can be expressed by first-order formulas in the language L containing the nonlogical symbols $\{<,=,+,*,||,0,1,\ldots\}$. Moreover, the formulas for pre'(S) and post'(S) can be written so that all free variables belong to Proof-var(S) , since pre'(S) and post'(S) depend only on the values of variables in Proof-var(S) . Similarly, the formula for I'(r) can be written so that all free variables belong to Proof-var(r) .

6.32. Definition: Let pre(S) , post(S) , and I(r) be first-order formulas of the language L which express pre'(S) , post'(S) , and I'(r) of Definition 6.31. The free variables in pre(S) and post(S) should belong to Proof-var(S) , and the free variables of I(r) should belong to Proof-var(r) .

6.2.3. Assertion Functions.

The functions pre, post, and I of Definition 6.32 are assertion functions for {P} T* {Q} . In order to prove this we must show that they satisfy Definition 4.15. Most of the requirements in this definition have the form $P_1 \vdash P_2$, where P_1 and P_2 are expressions involving pre, post, and I . In order to show $P_1 \vdash P_2$, i.e., that P_2 can be proved from P_1 using the deductive system D' of Theorem 6.19, we first show that $P_1 \Rightarrow P_2$ is a true statement about the natural numbers. Then P_1 can be proved from P_2 using D' , since D' is a complete proof system for the natural numbers.

The following theorem shows that for each formula $P_1 \vdash P_2$ of Definition 4.15, $P_1 \Rightarrow P_2$ is true.

<u>6.33. Theorem</u>: The (universal closures) of the following formulas are true for the natural numbers:

1. P $\Rightarrow$ pre(T*) and post(T*) $\Rightarrow$ Q
2. pre(S) $\Rightarrow$ post(S)^y_E for all assignments S (y:=E) in T*
3. pre(S) $\Rightarrow$ post(S) for all null S in T*
4. for all S = <u>begin</u> $S_1;\ldots;S_n$ <u>end</u> in T*
   a. pre(S) $\Rightarrow$ pre(S_1) and post(S_n) $\Rightarrow$ post(S)
   b. post(S_i) $\Rightarrow$ pre(S_{i-1}) , $1 \le i \le n-1$
5. for all S = <u>if</u> B <u>then</u> S_1 <u>else</u> S_2 in T*
   a. (pre(S) $\wedge$ B) $\Rightarrow$ pre(S_1) and (pre(S) $\wedge$ ¬B) $\Rightarrow$ pre(S_2)
   b. post(S_1) $\Rightarrow$ post(S) and post(S_2) $\Rightarrow$ post(S)
6. for all S = <u>while</u> B <u>do</u> S_1 in T*
   a. (pre(S) $\wedge$ B) $\Rightarrow$ pre(S_1)
   b. post(S_1) $\Rightarrow$ pre(S)
   c. (pre(S) $\wedge$ ¬B) $\Rightarrow$ post(S)

7. for all S = <u>with</u> r <u>when</u> B <u>do</u> S_1 in $T*$

   a. $(pre(S) \wedge B \wedge I(r)) \Rightarrow pre(S_1)$

   b. $post(S_1) \Rightarrow (post(S) \wedge I(r))$

8. for T_0 = L: <u>resource</u> $r_1,\ldots,r_M$: <u>cobegin</u> L_1: T_1 //...// L_N: T_N <u>coend</u>

   a. $pre(T_0) \Rightarrow (pre(T_1) \wedge\ldots\wedge pre(T_N) \wedge I(r_1) \wedge\ldots\wedge I(r_M))$

   b. $(post(T_1) \wedge\ldots\wedge post(T_N) \wedge I(r_1) \wedge\ldots\wedge I(r_M)) \Rightarrow post(T_0)$

<u>Proof</u>:

1. We must show $P[s] \Rightarrow pre(T*)[s]$, $post(T*)[s] \Rightarrow Q[s]$.

$pre(T*)[s] \equiv \exists\alpha, s_0$ such that $P[s_0]$=true and α is a computation for $T*$ with $T*$ current after α and $x[s]=x[value(s_0,\alpha)]\ \forall\ x$.

Letting α be empty and $s_0=s$, gives $P[s] \Rightarrow pre(T*)[s]$.

$post(T*)[s] \equiv \exists\alpha, s_0$ such that $P[s_0]$=true and α finishes $T*$ and $x[s]=x[value(s_0,\alpha)]\ \forall\ x$.

$\Rightarrow Q[s]$, since $\{P\}\ T*\ \{Q\}$ is true for the interpreter.

2.-6. The five sequential statements are treated in much the same way. As an example we show how to deal with assignment statements. If S is $y:=E$, we must show $pre(S) \Rightarrow post(S)^y_E$.

a. The case when S is not a proper component of the <u>cobegin</u> statement was given earlier.

b. Let S be a component of process T_k of the <u>cobegin</u> statement, and suppose s is a state such that $pre(S)[s]$ is true.

pre(S)[s] $\equiv \exists$ an acceptable local computation β for process T_k, with S current after β and $x[s]=x[value(\beta)]$ $\forall$ $x \in$ Proof-var(S), and for all $r \in$ resources(S), $\exists$ an acceptable resource computation γ_r for r with S current after γ_r and $x[s]=x[value(\gamma_r)]$ $\forall$ $x \in$ Proof-var(S).

Let $s'=s<y|E>$

$$\beta' = \beta(S, next(value(\beta), S))$$

$$\gamma_r' = \gamma_r(S, next(value(\gamma_r), S)) \quad \text{for} \quad r \in resources(S)$$

Now β' is an acceptable local computation for process T_k which finishes S, and $x[s']=x[value(\beta')]$ $\forall$ x Proof-var(S). (To check that β' is an acceptable local computation it is only necessary to verify 2a-c of Definition 6.27 for the new element (S,next(value(β),S)) in the sequence.)

For all $r \in$ resources(S), γ_r' is an acceptable resource computation which finishes S and has $x[s']=x[value(\gamma_r')]$ $\forall$ $x \in$ Proof-var(S). (To check this, it is only necessary to verify 3a-c of Definition 6.29 for the new element of the sequence.)

But this implies post(S)[s']=true, giving pre(S)[s] $\Rightarrow$ post(S)[s<y|E>] or pre(S) $\Rightarrow$ post$(S)^y_E$.

7. S is <u>with</u> r_0 <u>when</u> B <u>do</u> S_1, S in process T_k

   a. Assume s is a program state with $(pre(S) \wedge B \wedge I(r_0))[s]=true$.

Then $B[s]=\text{true} \wedge \exists$ an acceptable local computation β for process T_k with S current after β and $x[s]=x[\text{value}(\beta)]\ \forall\ x\varepsilon\text{Proof-var}(S)$, and $\forall\ r\varepsilon\text{resources}(S)$, $\exists$ an acceptable resource computation γ_r for r with S current after γ_r and $x[s]=x[\text{value}(\gamma_r)]\ \forall\ x\varepsilon\text{Proof-var}(S) \wedge \exists$ an acceptable resource computation γ for r_0 with the control of $\text{value}(\gamma)$ empty and $x[s]=x[\text{value}(\gamma)]\ \forall\ x\varepsilon\text{Proof-var}(r)$.

Let $\beta' = \beta(S,s_1)$, where s_1 is the state whose control part is the same as the control of $\text{next}(\text{value}(\beta),S)$, and whose variable part has $x[s_1]=x[s]\ \forall\ x$. Then β' is an acceptable local computation for process T_k (see 2a-c of Definition 6.27) with S_1 current after β' and $x[s]=x[\text{value}(\beta')]\ \forall\ x\varepsilon\text{Proof-var}(S_1)$.

For $r\varepsilon\text{resources}(S)$, let $\gamma_r' = \gamma_r(S,s_r)$, where the control of s_r = control of $\text{next}(\text{value}(\gamma_r),S)$, and $x[s_r]=x[s]\ \forall\ x$. Then γ_r' is an acceptable resource computation for r (see 3a-c of Definition 6.29) with S_1 current after γ_r' and $x[s]=x[\text{value}(\gamma_r')]\ \forall\ x\varepsilon\text{Proof-var}(S)$.

Finally, let $\gamma_{r_0}' = (S,s_2)$ where the control of s_2 is the single node S_1 and $x[s_2]=x[s]\ \forall\ x$. Then γ_{r_0}' is an acceptable resource computation for r_0 (see 2a-c of Definition 6.29) with S_1 current after γ_{r_0}' and $x[s]=x[\text{value}(\gamma_{r_0}')]\ \forall\ x\varepsilon\text{Proof-var}(S)$.

Thus $\exists\beta'$ and $\{\gamma_r':r\varepsilon\text{resources}(S_1)\ (=\text{resources}(S) \cup \{r_0\})\}$ which satisfy $\text{pre}'(S_1)(s)$, and $(\text{pre}(S) \wedge I(r) \wedge B) \Rightarrow \text{pre}(S_1)$.

b. Show $\text{post}(S_1) \Rightarrow (\text{post}(S) \wedge I(r_0))$

Suppose s is a program state with $\text{post}(S_1)[s]=\text{true}$. Then $\exists$ an acceptable local computation β for process T_k which finishes S_1, and $x[s]=x[\mathrm{value}(\beta)]$ $\forall$ $x\varepsilon$Proof-var(S) , and $\forall$ $r\varepsilon$resources(S_1) , $\exists$ an acceptable resource computation γ_r which finishes S_1 with $x[s]=x[\mathrm{value}(\gamma_r)]$ $\forall$ $x\varepsilon$Proof-var(S) .

Since α , γ_r finish S_1 , they also finish S . Also, since γ_{r_0} finishes S , the control of value(γ_{r_0}) is empty. Then $\exists$ an acceptable local computation β for process T_k which finishes S , and $x[s]=x[\mathrm{value}(\beta)]$ $\forall$ $x\varepsilon$Proof-var(S) (since Proof-var(S) $\subseteq$ Proof-var(S_1)), and $\forall$ $r\varepsilon$resources(S) (=resources(S_1) $\sim$ $\{r_0\}$) $\exists$ an acceptable resource computation γ_r which finishes S and has $x[s]=x[\mathrm{value}(\gamma_r)]$ $\forall$ $x\varepsilon$Proof-var(S) , and $\exists$ an acceptable resource computation γ_{r_0} with the control of value(γ_{r_0}) empty and $x[s]=x[\mathrm{value}(\gamma_{r_0})]$ $\forall$ $x\varepsilon$Proof-var(r_0) $\equiv$ post(S)[s] $\wedge$ I(r_0)[s] .

So post(S_1) $\Rightarrow$ (post(S) $\wedge$ I(r_0)) .

8. T_0 is the parallel statement

L_0: <u>resource</u> $r_1,\ldots,r_M$: <u>cobegin</u> L_1: T_1 //...// L_N: T_N <u>coend</u>

a. We must show that pre(T_0) $\Rightarrow$ (pre(T_1) $\wedge\ldots\wedge$ pre(T_N) $\wedge$ I(r_1) $\wedge\ldots\wedge$ I(r_M)) .

Suppose s is a program state with pre(T_0)[s]=true . Let s_k , $1\leq k\leq N$, be the state whose control part is the single node T_k and whose variable part has $x[s_k]=x[s]$ $\forall$ x . Let $\beta_k=s_k$. Then β_k is an acceptable local computation for T_k (β_k has initial state s_k and no statements executed) with T_k current after β_k and $x[s]=x[\mathrm{value}(\beta_k)]$ $\forall$ x . Thus, pre(T_k)[s]=true , $1\leq k\leq N$.

Next let s' be the program state whose control part is empty and variable part has $x[s]=x[s'] \ \forall \ x$. Let $\gamma_j = s'$, $1 \leq j \leq M$. Then γ_j is an acceptable resource computation for r_j (γ_j has initial state s' and no statements executed) with control of value(γ_j) empty and $x[s]=x[\text{value}(\gamma_j)] \ \forall \ x$. This gives $I(r_j)[s]=\text{true}$, $1 \leq j \leq M$. So $\text{pre}(T_0) \Rightarrow (\text{pre}(T_1) \wedge \ldots \wedge \text{pre}(T_N) \wedge I(r_1) \wedge \ldots \wedge I(r_M))$.

b. We must show

$$(\text{post}(T_1) \wedge \ldots \wedge \text{post}(T_N) \wedge I(r_1) \wedge \ldots \wedge I(r_M)) \Rightarrow \text{post}(T_0) .$$

Suppose s is a program state with

$$(\text{post}(T_1) \wedge \ldots \wedge \text{post}(T_N) \wedge I(r_1) \wedge \ldots \wedge I(r_M))[s]=\text{true} .$$

Then from $\text{post}(S_k)[s]$, $1 \leq k \leq N$, $\exists$ an acceptable local computation β_k which finishes S_k and has $x[s]=x[\text{value}(\beta_k)] \ \forall \ x \varepsilon \text{Proof-var}(T_k)$. From $I(r_j)[s]$, $1 \leq j \leq M$, $\exists$ an acceptable resource computation γ_j with the control of value(γ_j) empty and $x[s]=x[\text{value}(\gamma_j)] \ \forall \ x \varepsilon \text{Proof-var}(r_j)$.

To prove $\text{post}(T_0)[s]$ we need s_0, α such that

(*) { a. $P[s_0]=\text{true}$
b. α is a computation for T^* which finishes T_0
c. $x[s]=x[\text{value}(s_0,\alpha)] \ \forall \ x$.

s_0 and α can be derived from $\beta_1,\ldots,\beta_N$.

First, to find s_0 , let s_1 be the initial state of the local computation β_1 (any β_k , $1 \leq k \leq N$, would do). Since β_1 is acceptable, $pre(T_0)[s_1]=true$, i.e., $\exists s_0,\alpha_1$ such that $P[s_0]=true$, and α_1 is a computation for T* with T_0 current after α_1 and $x[s_1]=x[value(s_0,\alpha_1)]\ \forall\ x$.

This yields s_0 which satisfies a) above. For α , take $\alpha = \alpha_1 T_0 \alpha_2$, where α_2 is obtained by merging the statements of $\beta_1,\ldots,\beta_N$ Because of the auxiliary variables in T* it is possible to define α_2 so that the subsequence of α_2 consisting of statements from process T_k contains the same statements as β_k , while the subsequence of α_2 consisting of components of <u>withwhen</u> statements for resource r_j contains the same statements as γ_j . This is done by defining α_2 by merging the statements of $\beta_1,\ldots,\beta_N$ in a way which is consistent with the "time" at which statements were executed. More formally:

<u>6.34. Definition</u>: Let δ be a computation (standard, resource, or local) and S a statement from process T_k of T* .

If S occurs less than i times in δ , <u>time(S,i,δ)</u> = 0 .

If S occurs at least i times in δ , let s be the program state in δ just after the ith occurrence of S . Then

<u>time(S,i,δ)</u> = $L_k$time[s] , if S is not a <u>withwhen</u> statement
= $(1+\max[L_k time, r_j time))[s]$, if S is <u>with</u> r_j <u>when</u> B <u>do</u> S_1 .

Thus, time(S,i,δ) represents the "time" at which S was executed for the ith time in δ . In most cases "time" is given by the variable $L_k$time , but if S is a withwhen statement, the "time" for S is (1+max($L_k$time,$r_j$time)) , which will be assigned to $L_k$time as soon as the first statement of the critical section is executed.

6.35. Definition: Let α_2 be a sequence of statements obtained by merging the statements of $\beta_1,\ldots,\beta_N$ in a way which preserves the order of statements within a single β_k , and puts the ith occurrence of S from T_k before the jth occurrence of S' from T_m if time(S,i,β_k) < time(S',j,β_m) . (Since time is nondecreasing within β_k , these two requirements do not conflict.)

We must show $\alpha = \alpha_1 S \alpha_2$ satisfies b and c from (*) . The following lemma is the basis of the proof.

6.36. Lemma: $\alpha = \alpha_1 S \alpha_2$ is a computation for T* with

$$x[\text{value}(s_0,\alpha)]=x[\text{value}(\beta_k)] \ \forall \ x\varepsilon \text{var}(T_k) \ , \quad 1\leq k\leq N \ ,$$

$$x[\text{value}(s_0,\alpha)]=x[\text{value}(\gamma_j)] \ \forall \ x\varepsilon r_j \ , \quad 1\leq j\leq M \ .$$

Proof: Here we sketch the proof; a formal proof is given in Section 6.2.5. Basically, α yields the same values as β_k for the appropriate variables because α_2 executes statements from process T_k in the same order and with the same variable values as β_k . α_2 also executes statements for resource r_j in the same order and with the same variable values as γ_j .

It is clear from the definition of α_2 that it executes statements from T_k in the same order as β_k . To see that α_2 executes statements for resource r_j in the same order as γ_j, let L be a statement with r_j when B do S_1 in process T_k. Once L starts execution, the way in which it executes is determined by the variables in $var(S_1)$, since these are the only variables which can be used in S_1. The auxiliary variables L history x, $x \epsilon var(S_1)$, record these values each time L begins execution. Because

$$L\ history\ x[value(\beta_k)]=L\ history\ x[s]=L\ history\ x[value(\gamma_j)]\ ,$$

L is executed the same way in β_k and γ_j. This is true for each withwhen statement for r_j, so α_2, which is derived from the β's, contains the same statements as γ_j. Moreover, they have the same order in α_2 as in γ_j because "time" increases throughout γ_j, and statements in α_2 are ordered by "time".

To see that the final values of α_2 are those given in the lemma, let α_2' be an initial segment of α_2. Let β_k' and γ_j' be the corresponding initial segments of β_k and γ_j, $1 \leq k \leq N$, $1 \leq j \leq M$. Then by induction on the length of α_2',

$$x[value(s_0,\alpha_1 T_0 \alpha_2')]=x[value(\beta_k')]\ \forall\ x \epsilon var(T_k)\ ,$$

$$x[value(s_0,\alpha_1 T_0 \alpha_2')]=x[value(\gamma_j')]\ \forall\ x \epsilon r_j\ .$$

If α_2' is empty, $value(s_0,\alpha_1 T_0 \alpha_2')=value(\beta_1')=value(\beta_k')=value(\gamma_j')$, since all the β's and γ's start with the initial state given by L_0initial x[s]. If $\alpha_2' = \alpha_2''S$, where S is from process T_k, adding S to β_k" has the same effect as adding it to α_2" because the variables on which S operates are the same in both cases.

We observed when local and resource computations were defined that it is not always possible to find a program computation which is compatible with a given local or resource computation. The fact that we can find α_2 which is compatible with all the β's and γ's is due to the auxiliary variables of $T*$.

Given this lemma, b) and c) of (*) follow easily. b) is satisfied because α is a computation for $T*$ which finishes S (since each β_k finishes S_k). c) is satisfied because all the variables of $T*$ belong to some $var(T_k)$ or r_j (see the RPL syntax rules, Definition 4.3). If $x \in var(T_k)$, $x[value(s_0,\alpha)]=x[value(\beta_k)]=x[s]$. If $x \in r_j$, $x[value(s_0,\alpha)]=x[value(\gamma_j)]=x[s]$. So , $x[value(s_0,\alpha)]=x[s]$ for all x in $T*$. This establishes that s_0 and α satisfy a,b,c so $post(T_0)[s]=true$. Thus

$$(post(T_1) \wedge \ldots \wedge post(T_N) \wedge I(r_1) \wedge \ldots \wedge I(r_M)) \Rightarrow post(T_0) .$$

This finishes the proof of Theorem 6.33. We next show that pre, post, and I are assertion functions.

<u>6.37. Corollary</u>: Let D be the proof system consisting of A0-A7, and D' , a complete proof system for the natural numbers. Then pre, post, and I of Definition 6.32 are assertion functions for {P} T* {Q} .

Proof: We must show that pre, post, and I satisfy Definition 4.15. Most of the criteria are easily verified, since for each condition $P_1 \vdash P_2$ in the definition, $P_1 \Rightarrow P_2$ is true (Theorem 6.33) so that P_2 can be proved from P_1 using D' . Requirement 8c restricts the free variables in pre(S) and post(S) to elements of Proof-var(S) , and this is satisfied by Definition 6.32. Similarly, 8d restricts the free variables of I(r) to those in Proof-var(r) , and this requirement is also satisfied by Definition 6.32.

6.19. Theorem (Relative Completeness of RPL): If {P} T {Q} is true in the interpreter, where T is a program in a version of RPL whose data domain is the natural numbers with <,=,+,*, and || , then {P} T {Q} can be proved using A0-A8 and a complete proof system D' for the natural numbers.

Proof: Given T , first construct a program T* by adding auxiliary variables to T as done in Definition 6.22. Then by Corollary 6.24, {P} T* {Q} is also true for the interpreter. By Corollary 6.37, pre, post, and I of Definition 6.32 are assertion functions for {P} T* {Q} using the deductive system D' . Then by Theorem 4.16, there is a proof of {P} T* {Q} using D' , and by repeated applications of A8 the auxiliary variables can be removed to give a proof of {P} T {Q} .

6.2.4. Implications of the Relative Completeness Theorem.

Theorem 6.19 states that the RPL proof rules A0-A8 are relatively complete for programs which use the natural numbers and the operations of addition, multiplication, and concatenation. In this section, we generalize this result to programs with any of the usual data domains and then discuss the significance of relative completeness for proofs of program correctness.

Let us consider a program T in a language with data type(s) which include a set of values A and operations $\{o_1,\ldots,o_n\}$. This language may differ from the one of Theorem 6.19 both by failing to include the natural numbers with $\{<,=,+,*,||\}$ and by containing additional data values and operations.

First, suppose the language does not contain all of the natural numbers and $\{<,=,+,*,||\}$. This is a common case, as most real programming languages have only a finite subset of the natural numbers and do not include our kind of concatenation. The power of the natural numbers was required in the partial correctness proof for the statements which manipulate the "time" and "history" auxiliary variables. So we will simply expand the programming language to data types A' with operations $\{o_1,\ldots,o_m\}$ by adding $\{<,=,+,*,||,0,1,\ldots\}$, with the restriction that new operations and data values can only be used in statements for auxiliary variables.

If A' and $\{o_1,\ldots,o_m\}$ contain data types and operations which were not in the programming language of Theorem 6.19, there are two areas of concern. The first is the auxiliary variable L history x , which must be able to encode a sequence of values of x . We have shown how to encode a sequence of natural numbers, and the techniques can be applied to encode any sequence of values from an enumerable domain. If A' is an enumerable set, let $e:A' \rightarrow N$ be an enumeration of the elements of A'. A sequence $a_1,\ldots,a_k$ of values from A' can be represented by

$$(\ldots((o||e(a_1))||e(a_2))\ldots)||e(a_k) \ .$$

So by adding the operation $e()$ to M' (again to be used only with auxiliary variables), we can represent the auxiliary variables L history x .

The second problem is that it must be possible to express the assertions pre(S) , post(S) , and I(r) as first-order formulas over the domain of the programming language. This was possible when the language contained $\{<,=,+,*,||,0,1,\ldots\}$, because then the assertions represented recursively enumerable predicates. Now if A' is an enumerable set, and the operations $\{o_1,\ldots,o_m\}$ are recursive, the assertions for a program using A' and $\{o_1,\ldots,o_m\}$ are also recursively enumerable, and pre, post, and I can be expressed as first-order formulas.

This discussion leads to the following theorem.

<u>6.38. Theorem</u>: The proof-rules A0-A8 are relatively complete for programs in any version of RPL which has an enumerable domain and recursive operations.

<u>Proof</u>: The domain may be extended by adding the natural numbers, + , * , || , and e . Let D' be a complete proof system for this

extended domain. Then the proof of Theorem 6.19 (with the operations on L history modified as suggested above) becomes a proof of 6.38.

Since any implementable programming language must operate over an enumerable data domain with recursive operations, Theorem 6.38 implies the relative completeness of RPL for any reasonable choice of data types. This seems to indicate that A0-A8 are an adequate set of proof-rules in the sense that they capture all the information about program statements that is relevant for partial correctness. Since A0-A8 are not complete in the absolute sense, there are programs for which valid partial correctness formulas cannot be proved. Our main interest, however, is in proving the partial correctness of programs written by programmers who understand them and why they work. In such a case the programmer knows how to prove the necessary facts about the program domain. The relative completeness of A0-A8 implies that in this case it is possible to prove the program's partial correctness.

6.2.5. Proof of Lemma 6.31.

In Section 6.2.3 we gave an informal proof of Lemma 6.31. We now give a more detailed proof using four subsidiary lemmas. Recall that s is a program state with $post(T_0)[s]=true$; β_k is an acceptable local computation for process T_k , with $x[value(\beta_k)]=x[s]\ \forall\ x\epsilon var(T_k)$, $1\leq k\leq N$; γ_j is an acceptable resource computation for r_j with the control of $value(\gamma_j)$ empty and $x[value(\gamma_j)]=x[s]\ \forall\ x\epsilon var(\gamma_j)$; s_0,α_1 are defined in such a way that $pre(T_0)[value(s_0,\alpha_1)]=true$, and the initial state of β_1 is value(s_0,α_1) ; α_2 is a sequence of statements obtained by merging the statements of the β's in a way which preserves the "time" at which the statements were executed.

<u>6.39. Lemma</u>: The statements in α_2 for process T_k are in the same order as the statements of β_k .

<u>Proof</u>: Obvious from the definition of α_2 .

<u>6.40. Lemma</u>: If L: <u>with</u> r_j <u>when</u> B <u>do</u> S_1 is a statement in process T_k , L is executed in the same way in β_k as in γ_j , i.e., the subsequences of statements from L in β_k and γ_j are identical. Moreover, if β_k' is an initial segment of β_k which has S , a component of S_1 , current, and γ_j' is the corresponding initial segment of γ_j , then

$$x[\text{value}(\beta_k')]=x[\text{value}(\gamma_j')]\ \forall\ x\varepsilon\text{var}(S) .$$

<u>Proof</u>: Note that

$$\text{L history } x[\text{value}(\beta_k)]=\text{L history } x[s]=\text{L history } x[\text{value}(\gamma_j)] ,$$

$$\forall\ x\varepsilon\text{var}(S_1) , \text{ because } \text{L history } x\varepsilon\text{Proof-var}(T_k) \cap \text{Proof-var}(r_j) .$$

This means that L is executed the same number of times in β_k as in γ_j , and that each time the initial variable values are the same in both computations. If L does not properly contain any <u>withwhen</u> statements, this implies that L is executed in exactly the same way in β_k and γ_j , since the only variables accessible inside L are those in var(S_1) . If L does contain a <u>withwhen</u> statement L' for resource r_m , the L' history x variables record the value of' $x\varepsilon r_m$ when L' starts execution. Since L' history $x \varepsilon$ Proof-var(T_k) $\cap$ Proof-var(r_j) (L' history x is changed only within L , a <u>withwhen</u> statement for r_j)

L' history x[value(β_k)]=L' history x[s]=L' history x[value(γ_j)] ,

and β_k and γ_j obtain the same values for $x\varepsilon r_m$ when they start L'

Thus, β_k and γ_j execute statement L the same number of times, and each time they start with the same variable values; this implies that they execute L identically.

<u>6.41. Lemma</u>: The statements in α_2 for resource r_j are in the same order as the statements in γ_j .

<u>Proof</u>: The statements of α_2 come from the β_k's , $1 \leq k \leq N$. Each L: <u>with</u> r_j <u>when</u> B <u>do</u> S_1 in T_k is executed the same way in β_k and γ_j . So α_2 contains the same statements for r_j as γ_j does. They are in the same order because α_2 is ordered by "time". Recall that

$$\gamma_j = \gamma^1 \gamma^2 \ldots \gamma^n ,$$

where each γ^m is a subsequence which executes a <u>withwhen</u> statement for r_j . Now if S and S' occur in γ_j , with the ith occurrence of S before the kth occurrence of S' , either S and S' are in the same γ^m or time(S,i,γ_j) < time(S',k,γ_j) , because $r_j$time is updated at the end of each γ^m . By Lemma 6.40, time(S,i,γ_j) <

$time(S',k,\gamma_j)$ implies that $time(S,i,\beta_m) < time(S',k,\beta_n)$. Because the merging of statements from β which yields α_2 preserves both the order of statements from a single process and the time order, the ith occurrence of S precedes the jth occurrence of S' in α_2 .

6.42. Lemma: Let α_2' be an initial segment of α_2 , and β_k' , γ_j' , $1 \le j \le M$ be the corresponding initial segments of β_k , γ_j . Then

1. $\alpha' = \alpha_1 T_0 \alpha_2'$ is a computation for T^* .

2. a. $x[value(s_0,\alpha')]=x[value(\beta_k')]\ \forall\ x \varepsilon var(T_k)$, $1 \le k \le N$.

   b. if S is current after β_k' , S is current after α' .

3. $x[value(s_0,\alpha')]=x[value(\gamma_j')]\ \forall\ x \varepsilon r_j$, $1 \le j \le M$.

Proof: By induction on the length of α_2' .

If α_2' is empty:

1. $\alpha' = \alpha_1 T_0$ is a computation for T^* because α_1 is defined as a computation for T^* with T_0 current after α_1 .

2.a. By the definition of α_1 , $x[value(s_0,\alpha_1)]=x[value(\beta_1)]\ \forall\ x$. Now β_k , $1 \le k \le N$, is an acceptable local computation, so its initial state s_k satisfies $pre(T_0)$. This means that the time and history variables have the value 0 in s_k , and $\forall\ x \varepsilon var(T)$, $x[s_k]=$ L_0 initial $x[s_k]$ (the auxiliary variables receive these values just before L_0 begins). Since L_0 initial $x \varepsilon Proof\text{-}var(T_k)$, $1 \le k \le N$,

$$L_0 \text{ initial } x[value(\beta_k)]=L_0 \text{ initial } x[s] .$$

So all β_k's start with the same initial state, i.e.,

$$x[\text{value}(\beta_k')]=x[s_k]=x[s_1]=x[\text{value}(s_0,\alpha')] \ \forall\ x .$$

2.b. The only statement current after β_k' is T_k (see Definition 6.27), and T_k is also current after α' .

3. The initial state of each γ_j , $1\le j\le M$ is also identical to value(s_0,α') ; the proof is the same as for 2a.

Induction step: If $\alpha_2' = \alpha_2''S$, assume the lemma is satisfied for α_2'' and the corresponding β_k'' and γ_j'' . Let S belong to process T_k .

1. $\alpha' = \alpha_1 T_0 \alpha_2''S$ is a computation iff S is ready to execute after $\alpha'' = \alpha_1 T_0 \alpha_2''$. This requires two conditions to be satisfied.

   a. S is current after α'' . Since S is the next statement after β_k'' in β_k , S is current after β_k'' (see Definition 6.27). By 2a of the induction hypothesis this implies that S is current after α'' .

   b. If S is <u>with</u> r_j <u>when</u> B <u>do</u> S_1 , r_j is not busy in α_2'' and B[value(s_0,α'')]=true . Since γ_j finishes one <u>withwhen</u> statement before it starts another, and α_2 executes statements for r_j in the same order as γ_j , r_j is not busy in α_2'' . To see that B[value(s_0,α'')]=true , note that B[value(β_k')]=true by part 2b of Definition 6.27. Now

   $$x[\text{value}(s_0,\alpha_2'')]=x[\text{value}(\beta_k'')]\ \forall\ x\varepsilon\text{var}(S) \quad \text{(proved in 2 below)}$$

   $$=x[\text{value}(\beta_k')]\ \forall\ x\varepsilon\text{var}(S)\ ,\ \text{since S does not change any variable values.}$$

$$x[\text{value}(s_0,\alpha_2'')]=x[\text{value}(\gamma_j'')]\ \forall\ x\varepsilon r_j \quad \text{(induction)}$$

$$=x[\text{value}(\gamma_j')]\ \forall\ x\varepsilon r_j\ , \text{ since } S \text{ does not change any variable values}$$

$$=x[\text{value}(\beta_k')]\ \forall\ x\varepsilon r_j \quad \text{(Lemma 6.40)}$$

So $x[\text{value}(s_0,\alpha_2'')]=x[\text{value}(\beta_k')]\ \forall\ x\varepsilon \text{var}(S_1)$, and $B[\text{value}(s_0,\alpha_2'')]=\text{true}$.

2.a and b. S has the same effect in α_2'' as in β_k'' if all the variables in var(S) have the same values in both computations. Now

$$\text{var}(S) = \text{var}(T_k) \cup \left(\bigcup_{r\varepsilon \text{resources}(S)} r \right) .$$

By induction $x[\text{value}(s_0,\alpha'')]=x[\text{value}(\beta_k'')]\ \forall\ x\varepsilon \text{var}(T_k)$.
For $r_j\ \varepsilon$ resources(S) ,

$$x[\text{value}(s_0,\alpha'')] = x[\text{value}(\gamma_j'')]\ \forall\ x\varepsilon r_j \quad \text{(induction)}$$

$$= x[\text{value}(\beta_k'')]\ \forall\ x\varepsilon r_j \quad \text{(Lemma 6.40)}$$

3. If S is not a component of a <u>withwhen</u> statement for r_j , 3 is satisfied by induction, since S does not affect the variables of r_j .

If S is L: <u>with</u> r_j <u>when</u> B <u>do</u> S_1 , S does not change any variables when added to α'' and β_j'' , so again 3 is satisfied by induction.

If S is a proper component of L: <u>with</u> r_j <u>when</u> B <u>do</u> S_1 ,

$$x[\text{value}(s_0,\alpha'')] = x[\text{value}(\beta_k'')]\ \forall\ x\epsilon\text{var}(S) \quad \text{(proved in 2 above)}$$

$$= x[\text{value}(\gamma_j'')]\ \forall\ x\epsilon\text{var}(S) \quad \text{(Lemma 6.40)}$$

So S has the same effect on variables in α_2 and γ_j , yielding 3.

CHAPTER 7

CONCLUSIONS AND COMMENTS

In this thesis we have presented a method for verification of parallel programs. Our techniques are based on Hoare's axiomatic approach for proving partial correctness. We first provided axioms and inference rules for two parallel languages: a General Parallel Language and a Restricted Parallel Language. GPL is not a realistic programming language: it is introduced because it is powerful enough to represent most of the standard synchronizing operations. Thus, the deductive system for GPL can be used to establish the correctness of a program which uses semaphores, events, or any of the other common synchronizing tools. Unfortunately, these proofs may be quite complex because the verification of the interference-free property requires that each assertion be tested for invariance over each assignment statement from another process.

RPL avoids this complexity by restricting the use of shared variables to critical sections, so that only one process at a time has access to a particular variable. This gives RPL programs a structure which makes them easy to understand and to verify. In proving the correctness of an RPL program one must first define the invariant for each resource (possibly adding auxiliary variables to do so). The rest of the verification process requires only sequential reasoning, and is much simpler than a GPL proof.

The deductive systems for RPL and GPL are primarily intended for partial correctness proofs. However, a number of other properties are important for parallel programs, and the information obtained from a partial correctness proof can often be applied to verify that other properties also hold. In Chapter 5 we showed how the pre, post, and resource invariant assertions from a partial correctness proof can be used to establish mutual exclusion, freedom from deadlock, and program termination.

Finally, we evaluated the axioms and inference rules by defining interpreters for the languages RPL and GPL; the interpreters model the effect of executing programs on a real computer. The RPL and GPL deductive systems were shown to be consistent with the interpreters, i.e., they accurately describe the effects of program execution. For RPL we also showed that the deductive system was relatively complete with respect to the interpreter, i.e., given adequate knowledge about the data domain of the program, any true partial correctness formula can be proved. Thus, the axioms and inference rules do not omit any crucial information about program execution.

Our results suggest several directions for future work. One important task is the extension of the deductive system to a more powerful programming language. A major weakness of RPL and GPL is that both are limited to programs with a fixed degree of parallelism. Parallel execution is initiated by the cobegin statement, which starts a fixed number of parallel processes. The addition of recursive procedures would overcome this limitation, since a recursive procedure which contained a cobegin statement could create an arbitrary number of parallel processes. We conjecture that recursive procedures would increase the complexity of partial correctness proofs only as much as in the sequential case, i.e., a new rule describing recursion must be added, but no change in the existing axioms is necessary. However, mutual exclusion and deadlock proof techniques may require more significant modification.

More generally, it is clear that neither RPL nor GPL is a perfect language for parallel programming. GPL is too powerful to be feasible for implementation, and it does not provide enough structure to aid the programmer in organizing his program. Although RPL is an improvement in both these areas, the conditional critical section is still somewhat inefficient as a synchronizing operation. Moreover, there are some problems which do not fit reasonably into the RPL framework -- for example the readers and writers problem discussed in Chapter 5. There is a need for new language constructions which can be implemented efficiently and which provide a basis for organizing programs in a clear and easily verified manner.

Another area in which further work is needed is the verification of properties other than partial correctness. Although techniques were presented in Chapter 5 for proving some of these properties, there are many more to consider, e.g., priority scheduling and progress for each process. Not all of these properties will be amenable to the axiomatic approach (see the discussion at the end of Chapter 5), but the range of properties which can be verified using this and other techniques can certainly be extended.

Finally, the results of this thesis should be very applicable to automatic program verification. We visualize an approach in which the programmer works with an interactive system, like the one described by Good, et al. [Go75]. He first gives his program, possibly with auxiliary variables, and defines resource and loop invariants. The verification system is then left with the mechanical problem of checking whether the invariants and input and output conditions are consistent. It may respond that they are consistent, thus establishing the correctness of the program; that they are inconsistent, implying an error in either the program or the invariants; or that there is insufficient information to decide. In the last case the programmer can provide more information by adding auxiliary variables or strengthening the invariants.

BIBLIOGRAPHY

[As71] Ashcroft, E.A. and Z. Manna. Formalization of Properties of Parallel Programs. Machine Intelligence 6, pp. 17-41, University of Edinburgh Press, 1971.

[As73] Ashcroft, E.A. Proving Assertions about Parallel Programs. Technical Report CS-73-01. Department of Applied Analysis and Computer Science, University of Waterloo, 1973.

[Br72a] Brinch Hansen, P. A Comparison of Two Synchronizing Concepts. Acta Informatica 1, pp. 190-199, 1972.

[Br72b] ----- Structured Multiprogramming. CACM 15:7, pp. 574-578, 1972.

[Br73] ----- Concurrent Programming Concepts. Computing Surveys 5:4, pp. 223-245, 1973.

[Br74] ----- Concurrent Pascal: A Programming Language for Operating Systems Design. Information Sciences Technical Report 10, California Institute of Technology, 1974.

[Ca73] Cadiou, J.M. and J.J. Lévy. Mechanizable Proofs about Parallel Processes. Proc. 14th Annual IEEE Symposium on Switching and Automata Theory, pp. 34-48, 1973.

[Co71] Courtois, P.J., R. Heymans, and D.L. Parnas. Concurrent Control with "Readers" and "Writers". CACM 14:10, pp. 667-668, 1971.

[Co75] Cook, S.A. Axiomatic and Interpretive Semantics for an Algol Fragment. Technical Report 79, Department of Computer Science, University of Toronto, 1975.

[Di68a] Dijkstra, E.W. Co-operating Sequential Processes, in F. Genuys, ed. Programming Languages NATO Advanced Study Institute, pp. 43-112, Academic Press, 1968.

[Di68b] ----- The Structure of the THE Multiprogramming System. CACM 11:5, pp. 341-347, 1968.

[Di70] ----- Notes on Structured Programming. Technical University of Eindhoven Report EWD249. Eindhoven, Netherlands, 1970.

[Di71] ----- Hierarchical Ordering of Sequential Processes, in Hoare and Perrott, ed. Operating Systems Techniques, Academic Press, 1972.

[Di73] Dijkstra, E.W. A Simple Axiomatic Basis for Programming Language Constructs. Lecture notes from the International Summer School on Structured Programming and Programmed Structures, Munich, Germany, 1973.

[Fl67] Floyd, R.W. Assigning Meaning to Programs, in Schwartz, J.T., ed. Mathematical Aspects of Computer Science Proc. Symposia in Applied Mathematics 19, pp. 19-32, Amer. Math. Soc., 1967.

[Go75] Good, I., R.L. London, and W.W. Bledsoe. An Interactive Program Verification System. IEEE Transactions on Software Engineering 1:1, pp. 59-67, 1975.

[Ha72] Habermann, A.N. Synchronization of Communicating Processes. CACM 15:3, pp. 171-176, 1972.

[Ho69] Hoare, C.A.R. An Axiomatic Basis for Computer Programming. CACM 12:10, pp. 576-580, 1969.

[Ho72] ----- Towards a Theory of Parallel Programming, in Hoare and Perrott, ed. Operating Systems Techniques, Academic Press, 1972.

[Ho74a] ----- Monitors: An Operating System Structuring Concept. CACM 17:10, pp. 548-557, 1974.

[Ho74b] Hoare, C.A.R. and P.E. Lauer. Consistent and Complementary Formal Theories of the Semantics of Programming Languages. Acta Informatica 3, pp. 135-153, 1974.

[La71] Lauer, P.E. Consistent Formal Theories of the Semantics of Programming Languages. IBM Labroatory Vienna TR 25.121, 1971.

[La73] Lauer, H.C. Correctness in Operating Systems. Ph.D. thesis, Carnegie-Mellon University, 1973.

[Li74a] Lipton, R.J. On Synchronization Primitive Systems. Ph.D. thesis, Carnegie-Mellon University, 1974.

[Li74b] ----- Reduction: A New Method for Proving Properties of Systems of Processes. Yale Computer Science Research Report 30, 1974.

[Ma74] Manna, Z. and A. Pnueli. Axiomatic Approach to Total Correctness of Programs. Acta Informatica 3, pp. 243-263, 1974.

[Mi72] Milner, R. and R.W. Weyrauch. Proving Compiler Correctness in a Mechanized Logic. Machine Intelligence 7, pp. 51-70, Edinburgh University Press, 1972.

[Ne74] Newton, G. Proving Properties of Interacting Processes. Computer Science Technical Report 74-9, University of Washington, 1974.

[Ro74] Rosen, B.K. Correctness of Parallel Programs: The Church-Rosser Approach. IBM Research Report RC5107. Thomas J. Watson Research Center, Yorktown Heights, New York, 1974.

[Si75] Sintzoff, M. and A. van Lamsweerde. Constructing Correct and Efficient Concurrent Programs. Proc. ACM-IEEE International Conference on Reliable Software, 1975.